Celebrate the Months
APRIL

EDITOR:
Joellyn Thrall Cicciarelli

ILLUSTRATORS:
Darcy Tom
Jana Travers
Jane Yamada

PROJECT DIRECTOR:
Carolea Williams

CONTRIBUTING WRITERS:

Cindy Barden	Judy Herz
Rosa Drew	Kathy Hiatt
Trisha Callella	Kimberly Jordano
Rhonda Erickson	Mary Kurth

TABLE OF CONTENTS

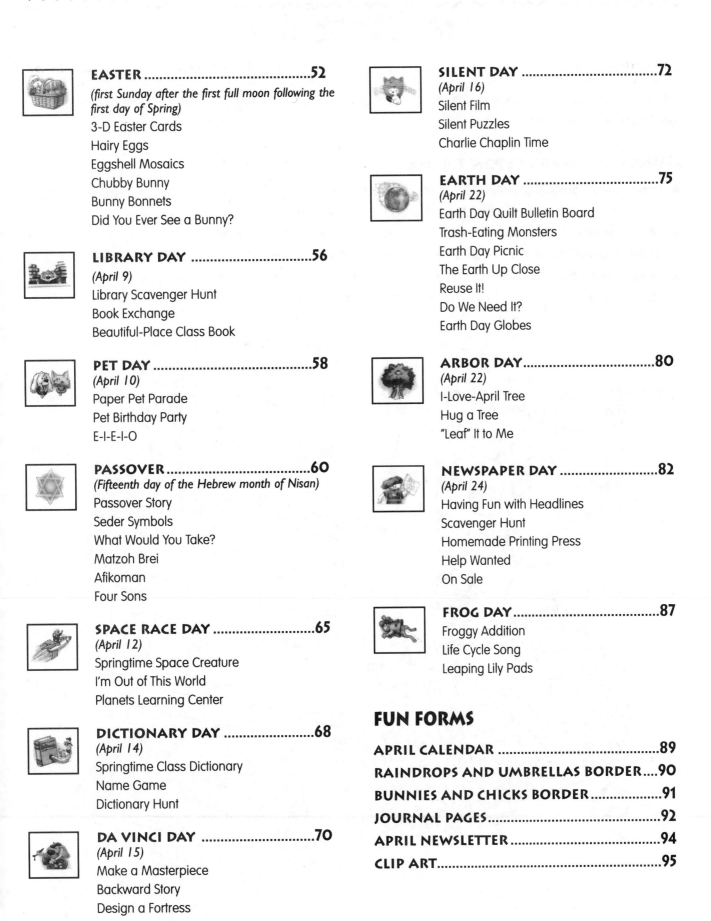

INTRODUCTION

Seasons, holidays, annual events, and just-for-fun monthly themes provide fitting frameworks for learning! Celebrate April and its special days with these exciting and unique activities. This activity book of integrated curriculum activities includes the following:

MONTHLY CELEBRATION THEMES

▲ **monthly celebration activities** that relate to monthlong and weeklong events or themes such as Rainy Days, Bicycle Safety Week, and Keep America Beautiful Month.

▲ **literature lists** of fiction and nonfiction books for each monthly celebration.

▲ **bulletin-board displays** that can be used for seasonal decoration and interactive learning-center fun.

▲ **take-home activities** that reinforce what is being taught in school, encourage home–school communication, and help children connect home and school learning.

SPECIAL-DAY THEMES

▲ **special-day activities** that relate to 15 special April days, including April Fool's Day, Earth Day, and Library Day. Activities integrate art, songs and chants, language arts, math, science, and social studies.

▲ **calendar cards** that complement each of the 15 special days and add some extra seasonal fun to your daily calendar time.

▲ **literature lists** of fiction and nonfiction books for each special day.

FUN FORMS

▲ a **blank monthly calendar** for writing lesson plans, dates to remember, special events, book titles, new words, incentives, and math and calendar activities.

▲ **seasonal border pages** that add eye-catching appeal to parent notes, homework assignments, letters, certificates, announcements, and bulletins.

▲ **seasonal journal pages** for students to share thoughts, feelings, stories, or experiences. Reproduce and bind several pages for individual journals or combine single, completed journal pages to make a class book.

▲ a **classroom newsletter** for students to report current classroom events and share illustrations, comics, stories, or poems. Reproduce and send completed newsletters home to keep families informed and involved.

▲ **clip art** to add a seasonal flair to bulletin boards, class projects, charts, and parent notes.

SPECIAL-DAY CALENDAR CARD ACTIVITIES

Below are a variety of ways to introduce special-day calendar cards into your curriculum.

PATTERNING

During daily calendar time, use one of these patterning activities to reinforce students' math skills.

▲ Use special-day calendar cards and your own calendar markers to create a pattern for the month, such as regular day, regular day, special day.

▲ Number special-day cards in advance. Use only even- or odd-numbered special days for patterning. (Create your own "special days" with the blank calendar cards.) Use your own calendar markers to create the other half of the pattern.

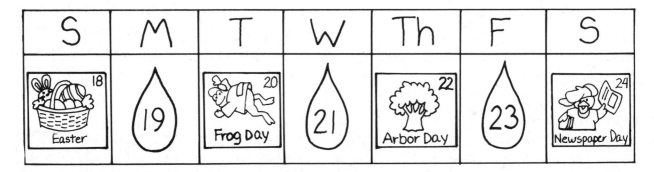

▲ At the beginning of the month, attach the special-day cards to the calendar. Use your own calendar markers for patterning. When a special day arrives, invite a student to remove the special-day card and replace it with your calendar marker to continue the pattern.

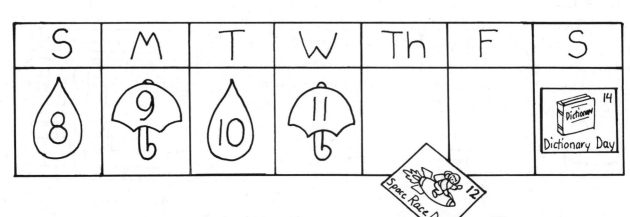

HIDE AND FIND

On the first day of the month, hide numbered special-day cards around the classroom. Invite students to find them and bring them to the calendar area. Have a student volunteer hang each card in the correct calendar space as you explain the card's significance.

A FESTIVE INTRODUCTION

On the first day of the month, display special-day cards in a festive setting such as a baby animal display. Invite students, one at a time, to remove a card and attach it to the calendar as you explain its significance.

POCKET-CHART SENTENCE STRIPS

On the first day of the month, have the class dictate a sentence to correspond with each special-day card. For example, on April Fool's Day you might write *On this special day, we try to trick people.* Put the sentence strips away. When a special day arrives, place the corresponding strip in a pocket chart next to the calendar. Move a fun "pointer" (such as a rubber chicken) under the words, and have students read the sentence aloud. Add sentences to the pocket chart on each special day.

GUESS WHAT I HAVE

Discuss the special days and give each student a photocopy of one of the special-day cards. (Two or three students may have the same card.) Have students take turns describing their card without revealing the special day. For example, a student may say, "This is the day Jewish people celebrate their freedom." Invite the student who guesses Passover to attach the card to the calendar.

TREAT BAGS

Place each special-day card and a small corresponding treat or prize in a resealable plastic bag. For example, place a plastic rocket in a bag for Space Race Day. On the first day of the month, pin the bags on a bulletin board near the calendar. Remove the special-day cards from the bags and attach them to the calendar as you discuss each day. As a special day arrives, remove and explain the corresponding bag's contents. Choose a student to keep the contents as a special reward.

LITERATURE MATCHUP

Have students sit in two lines facing each other. Provide each member of one group with a special-day card and each member of the other group with books whose subjects match the special-day cards held by the other group. Invite students to match cards and books, come forward in pairs, and introduce the day and book. Display the books near the calendar for students to read.

MINI-BOOKS

Reproduce numbered special-day cards so each student has a set. Have students sequence and staple their cards to make mini-books. Invite students to read the books and take them home to share with family members.

CREATIVE WRITING

Have each student glue a copy of a special-day card to a piece of construction paper. Invite students to illustrate and write about the special days. Have students share their writing. Display the writing near the calendar.

LUNCH SACK GAME

Provide each student with a paper lunch sack, a photocopy of each special-day card, and 15 index cards. Have students decorate the bags for the month. Invite students to color the special-day cards and write on separate index cards a word or sentence describing each day. Have students place the special-day cards and index cards in the bags. Ask students to trade bags, empty the contents, and match index cards to special-day cards.

SPECIAL-DAY BOX

One week before a special day, provide each student with a photocopied special-day card, an empty check box or shoebox, and a four-page square blank book. Ask each student to take the box, book, and card home to prepare a special-day box presentation. Have students write about their special day on the four book pages and place in the box small pictures or artifacts relating to the day. Ask students to decorate the boxes and glue their special-day cards to the top. Have students bring the completed boxes to school on the special day and give their presentations as an introduction to the day.

RAINY DAYS

April showers bring May flowers! Welcome April rains and the flowers they bring with some wet-and-wild rainy-day activities— they'll make a big splash!

RAINY WORDS BULLETIN BOARD

Read *Rain Drop Splash* aloud. After story discussion, invite students to brainstorm rain-related words such as *pour, splash, puddle, trickle, sprinkle, torrent, raindrop, drip, soaked, drenched, wet,* and *muggy*. Show students how to fold a piece of light-blue construction paper in half and cut a symmetrical raindrop. Ask each student to choose a rain-related word and write it on the raindrop. Have students trace their raindrops on aluminum foil, cut them out, and glue the foil drops to the back of the originals. Cut a large umbrella shape (top half) from butcher paper. Gather the top to a point and fold the sides in about an inch (2.5 cm). Staple the sides to the bulletin board so the umbrella curves out, creating a three-dimensional display. Attach two construction-paper boots under the umbrella. Invite half the students to attach fishing line to their raindrops. Hang them from the ceiling near the bulletin board and staple the rest of the raindrops to the board's background. Add the title *It's Raining Rainy Words!* Have students use the words when writing April stories and poems.

MATERIALS
▲ *Rain Drop Splash* by Alvin R. Tresselt
▲ light-blue construction paper
▲ scissors
▲ crayons or markers
▲ aluminum foil
▲ glue
▲ butcher paper
▲ construction-paper boots
▲ stapler
▲ fishing line

RAIN ON EVERYTHING

Read *Rain* aloud. After story discussion, have students cut raindrop shapes from construction paper. Have students complete the sentence *Rain on the _____!* on the raindrop and illustrate their sentence. Encourage students to think of unique phrases such as *Rain on the picnic!* Compile the pages in a raindrop-shaped class book titled *Rain on Everything!*

WHAT MAKES IT RAIN?

Read *What Makes it Rain? The Story of a Raindrop* aloud. After discussion, demonstrate the water cycle. Heat water in an electric skillet. Hold a cookie sheet filled with ice about 12" (31 cm) above the water. Explain that the heat represents heat from the sun, the skillet represents the earth, and the cookie sheet represents the sky (the cooler, upper atmosphere). In two to three minutes, the water from the pan will become water vapor and rise. (Explain that in nature, the sun's heat causes water to evaporate from the ground.) The water vapor rises until it reaches the cookie sheet, where it condenses into a liquid. (Explain that in nature, the rising water condenses and becomes clouds in the sky.) As condensation continues, the water droplets on the cookie sheet get bigger and heavier until they fall back into the pan. (Explain that in nature, the falling water droplets are rain.) Explain that once the water is back in the pan, the process begins again (just like in nature).

TELL ME ABOUT THE RAIN

MATERIALS

▲ crayons

▲ construction paper

▲ scissors

▲ blue water "wash" (one cup water mixed with one tablespoon blue tempera paint)

▲ paintbrushes

▲ glue

▲ Styrofoam packing "peanuts"

▲ blank cassette tape

▲ cassette recorder and player

Invite each student to draw and color a rainy-day scene on construction paper. Ask students to make construction-paper cutouts, such as children, umbrellas, clouds, and raindrops, to add to their pictures. Have students paint over the scenes with a blue water "wash." When the cutouts are dry, ask students to glue them to Styrofoam packing "peanuts" and then glue the peanuts to their scenes to create a three-dimensional effect. Write a different number on each picture and hang them. Invite each student to explain his or her design on a cassette and say the design's number. Invite students to look at the scenes, listen to the tape recording, and guess artists' names, as a listening center activity.

RAIN GAUGE

MATERIALS

▲ Rain Gauge Calendar Pattern reproducible (page 14)

▲ April calendar

▲ 2-liter, flat-bottom plastic soda bottle

▲ craft knife

▲ permanent marker

▲ centimeter ruler

▲ crayons

Copy a rain gauge pattern for each day of the month and display the patterns near an April calendar. Make a rain gauge. Cut off the top four inches of a 2-liter soda bottle. Starting at the bottom of the bottle, mark centimeter lines with a permanent marker. On the first day of April, have students place the rain gauge outside so it is exposed to rainfall but protected from wind. Each afternoon, invite volunteers to check the gauge and count the number of centimeters of rain that fell that day. Ask other volunteers to go to the calendar and graph the rainfall on that day's rain gauge pattern with crayons. Continue the activity each day of the month. For extra fun, develop counting, estimating, and comparing activities using the rain gauge patterns.

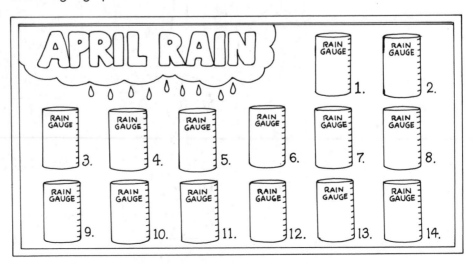

UNDER THE UMBRELLA

Prepare 40 construction-paper raindrops and print a different question dealing with a current topic of study on each. Suspend an open umbrella from a coatrack so it looks like a lamp shade. Attach a string to each of the eight umbrella points. Clip eight raindrop questions to the strings with clothespins. On the morning of the first day of this activity, invite eight students to remove a raindrop and, during the day, find the answer to the question on it. At the end of the day, invite the eight players to share their questions and answers. Continue the game for four more days until the students have answered all 40 questions.

SPIN THE UMBRELLA

Write rain-related tasks on separate index cards, one task for each student. Rain-related tasks could include *Name three words that rhyme with* rain; *Spell* rain *forward and backward; Name one word with the word* rain *in it;* or *Name a word that means the same as* rain. Open an umbrella, turn it over, and place the cards inside. Tape an index card labeled *Your Turn* to one umbrella point. Have students stand in a large circle around the umbrella. Invite a volunteer to spin the umbrella. When the umbrella stops spinning, ask the student standing across from the *Your Turn* card to choose a card from the umbrella and complete the task. (Offer help if necessary.) Ask that student to spin the umbrella and sit down. Play Spin the Umbrella until each student has had a turn.

IN-THE-RAIN WATERCOLORS

Invite students to brainstorm interesting water-related scenes such as an ocean, a rainy day in the park, or a crying face. Have each student use watercolor paints to paint a scene. Tell students to pretend they have left their painting out in the rain. Invite students to simulate rain by spraying the paintings with water until the images become muted. Discuss the changes in the paintings. When dry, display under the heading *In-the-Rain Watercolors*.

RAINY DAY GAMES

HOME ACTIVITY

Send home a resealable plastic bag, an index card, and a letter asking students and their families to create and send back (in the bag) a rainy-day "indoor recess" game to share. Offer game suggestions, such as homemade board games with questions and dice, homemade checkerboards with button markers, or exploration kits (magnets, rocks, stamps, etc.) with information cards (index cards) that explain the contents. Invite students to bring in their game bags on a designated day and share how to play the games. Place the games in a box labeled Rainy Day Games and invite students to use them during indoor recess.

RAIN GAUGE CALENDAR PATTERN

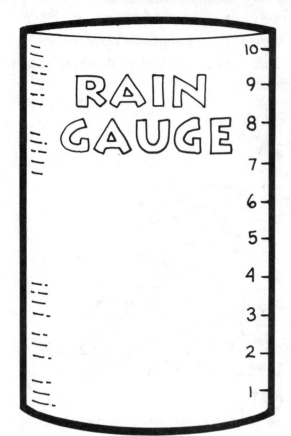

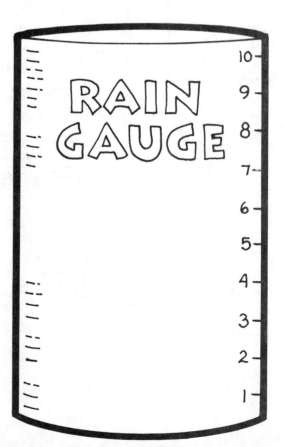

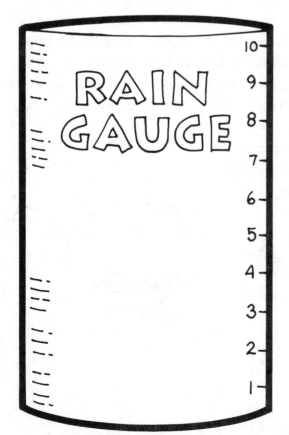

BABY ANIMALS

In spring, animals of the world welcome their young. Join the animals in celebrating the arrival of their young ones with the following baby animal activities— these fun activities are just waiting to be hatched!

LITERATURE LINKS

Across the Stream
by Mirra Ginsburg

Are You My Mother?
by P.D. Eastman

Bunches and Bunches of Bunnies
by Louise Matthews

The Chick and the Duckling
by Mirra Ginsburg

Chickens Aren't the Only Ones
by Ruth Heller

Egg to Chick
by Millicent E. Selsam

Have You Seen My Duckling?
by Nancy Tafuri

Make Way for Ducklings
by Robert McCloskey

Over in the Meadow
by Ezra Jack Keets

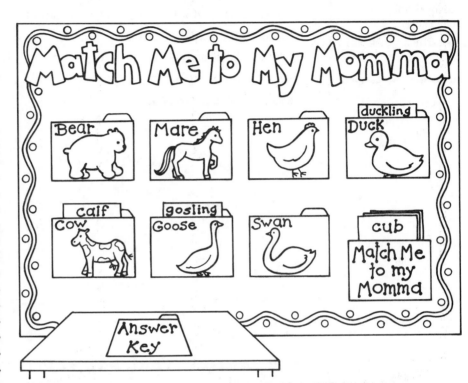

MATCH ME TO MY MOMMA BULLETIN BOARD

Cut out several adult and baby animal pictures from magazines, such as mare/foal, cow/calf, duck/duckling, goose/gosling, bear/cub, hen/chick, and swan/signet. Separate the adult pictures from the baby pictures. Glue each adult animal picture to a file folder and write the adult animal name under the picture. Staple the sides of each folder to make a pocket. Arrange the file folders on a bulletin board, showing the adult names and pictures. Write a baby animal name for each adult animal on individual pieces of tagboard. Place the baby names in a file folder labeled *Match Me to My Momma.* Staple the folder like a pocket to the bulletin board. To create an answer key, glue each baby animal picture to a piece of construction paper and write its name and the matching adult name under the picture. Place the answer key in a folder near the bulletin board. Add the title *Match Me to My Momma.* Invite students to visit the board and match babies to adults by placing baby animal names in the adult animal folders. Have students self-check by looking at the baby animal pictures and names in the answer key.

MATERIALS
▲ scissors
▲ adult and baby animal pictures (from magazines)
▲ glue
▲ file folders
▲ marker
▲ stapler
▲ tagboard
▲ construction paper

BABY ANIMAL MATH STORIES

MATERIALS
- ▲ slips of paper
- ▲ container
- ▲ construction paper
- ▲ crayons or markers
- ▲ counters (raisins, buttons, etc.)
- ▲ bookbinding materials

Write a different animal name on separate slips of paper, one for each student. Place the names in a container. Invite each student to choose a name and think of a "math story" that incorporates that animal and its babies. (For example, *A mother owl was hunting with three babies. Two got lost in the trees. How many babies finished hunting with their mother?*) Invite students to illustrate their stories on construction paper and write answers on the back. Help students write their stories under the illustrations. Ask each student to share his or her story as the class solves the problem using counters such as raisins or buttons. Bind the stories in a class book titled *Baby Math Stories*.

BABY ANIMAL YARN PROJECTS

MATERIALS
- ▲ 5" (12.5 cm) cardboard squares
- ▲ black crayon
- ▲ glue
- ▲ yarn strands
- ▲ construction paper

Invite each student to draw a black-crayon outline of a favorite baby animal in the center of a cardboard square. Have students spread glue around the outlines. Ask students to press yarn strands, one at a time, into the glue to fill in the outline, following the shape's curves and angles. Invite each student to create a border of yarn strands around the perimeter. Have each student finish the project by spreading glue in the open spaces between the animal and the border and laying down strands until all of the cardboard is covered. Invite each student to use yarn and glue to "write" the animal's name on a construction-paper strip. Display the animals with the heading *We Love Baby Animals!*

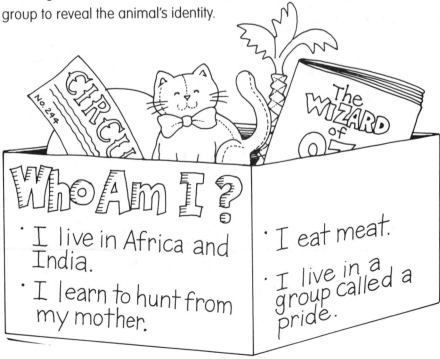

MATERIALS
▲ slips of paper

BABY TALK

Invite students to share and agree on four baby animal sounds such as the sound made by a chick (*peep, peep*), kitten (*mew*), puppy (*yipe*), and foal (*whinny*). Write each animal name on at least five slips of paper, one for each student. Have students choose an animal name and keep its identity a secret. Then have them stand in a large playing area and close their eyes. At a signal, ask students to make their animal noise and roam around until they find all the other students who are making the same noise. When students are in groups, have them open their eyes and sit down. Ask questions such as *How did you feel wandering around with your eyes closed? What was it like to finally find someone like you? How did your group stay together? Why do you think animals stay together in groups?*

MATERIALS
▲ index cards
▲ medium-size cardboard boxes
▲ animal books, magazines, posters, photographs, and videotapes
▲ art supplies (construction paper, crayons or markers, glue, scissors, feathers, pipe cleaners, twigs, felt)
▲ writing paper

WHO AM I? BOXES

Write a different baby animal name on each of five index cards. Divide the class into five groups, giving each group a card. Tell groups they will be preparing a *Who Am I?* box for the baby animal whose name appears on their card. Explain that a *Who Am I?* box contains artifacts, "found objects," and artwork that give clues to an animal's identity without revealing it. Explain that the outside of the box is covered with facts that also give clues to the animal's identity. Assign an older student or adult volunteer to help each group. Provide groups with books, magazines, posters, photographs, and videotapes about their animals. Ask each group to use the information and prepare a *Who Am I?* box. Number the finished boxes and place each on a different table. Invite another class to visit. Split the visiting class into five groups. Have the visiting groups rotate to each box, examine it, and write a guess for each animal's identity. After rotation, invite each *Who Am I?* group to reveal the animal's identity.

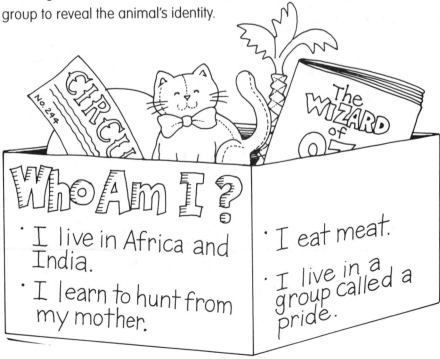

Who Am I?
· I live in Africa and India.
· I learn to hunt from my mother.
· I eat meat.
· I live in a group called a pride.

MATERIALS
▲ none

POP-UP POETRY—PART ONE

Teach students the following poem and motions. Have students practice and perform the poem for other classes or parents. Follow up by having students make the chicks described below.

Tap, Tap, Tap	**Motions**
Tap, tap, tap.	*Students knock in the air.*
I see a beak.	*Students form a beak with their hands.*
Tap, tap, tap.	*Students knock in the air.*
I hear a peep.	*Students cup their ears.*
Tap, tap, tap.	*Students knock in the air.*
The time is near.	*Students tap imaginary watches.*
Tap, tap, tap.	*Students crouch down and knock.*
A chick is here!	*Students jump in the air.*

MATERIALS
▲ glue
▲ yellow construction-paper circles
▲ large white construction-paper ovals
▲ brass fasteners
▲ wiggly eyes
▲ candy corn
▲ yellow feathers (available at craft stores)

POP-UP POETRY—PART TWO

Complete this activity after students know and have performed "Tap, Tap, Tap" (above). Have each student glue two yellow construction-paper circles on top of each other to make a chick body. Ask each student to cut the large white oval in half horizontally to make a hatching egg. Have each student slightly overlap the oval halves and insert a brass fastener to the left side as a hinge so the egg opens and closes. Have each student glue the chick body behind the egg bottom so the chick is revealed when the top part of the egg is moved up. Have each student glue on wiggly eyes, a candy-corn beak, and yellow feathers. Ask students to copy "Tap, Tap, Tap" on the eggs.

Tap, Tap, Tap

Tap, tap, tap.
I see a beak.
Tap, tap, tap.
I hear a peep.
Tap, tap, tap.
The time is near.
Tap, tap, tap.
A chick is here.

DUCKLINGS STORY SEQUENCE

MATERIALS

▲ *Make Way for Ducklings* by Robert McCloskey

▲ butcher paper

▲ crayons or markers

Read *Make Way for Ducklings* aloud. As a class, retrace the ducklings' steps and list the landmarks they passed as they went home with their mother. Divide the class into groups, one group for each listed step. Have each group illustrate the step on butcher paper. Rearrange the classroom to make a trail between desks for "ducklings" to follow. Hang each group's illustration along the trail in the order it occurred in the story. Have each group stand near its illustration and practice a sentence to explain it, such as *Then the ducklings* _____. Invite another class to become "ducklings" and follow the story trail. Have the class begin at the first illustration, look at it, listen to the group's sentence, and move along the trail.

BABIES-FROM-EGGS HOMEWORK BASKET

MATERIALS

▲ *Chickens Aren't the Only Ones* by Ruth Heller

▲ plastic or paper grass

▲ plastic eggs

▲ plastic animals

▲ Homework Basket reproducible (page 20)

▲ basket

▲ bookbinding materials

HOME ACTIVITY

Place *Chickens Aren't the Only Ones*, plastic or paper grass, several plastic eggs (each with a plastic animal inside), and a Homework Basket reproducible in a basket. Include plastic animals that hatch from eggs, such as dinosaurs, birds, crocodiles, and snakes, and those that do not, such as whales, bears, pigs, and cows. Each day in April, send the basket home with a different student. Ask students and family members to complete the activity and return the basket the next day. At the end of the month, compile the journal entries into a class book.

~~~~~~

HOMEWORK BASKET

Dear Family,

My class is celebrating baby animals this month. Please complete the following activity with me so I can learn about baby animals that hatch from eggs. Thank you!

1. Read the story and discuss it.

2. Carefully open each egg and discuss if the animal inside hatches from an egg in "real life" or if it is born alive.

3. Complete the journal entry below.

4. Have an "egg-citing" time, and return all items tomorrow for another student to enjoy!

JOURNAL PAGE

My favorite animal that hatches from an egg is_____.

I like it because _____

_____

One thing I learned from the book is _____

_____

Here is a picture of something I learned:

April © 1997 Creative Teaching Press

KEEP AMERICA BEAUTIFUL MONTH

As trees bud and flowers bloom, April reminds us of the fragile beauty of our land—and our responsibility to preserve it. Help your students understand the importance of "keeping America beautiful" with the following activities. The activities are fun, easy-to-manage, and best of all, "environmentally friendly"!

LITERATURE LINKS

The Earth Is Painted Green
by Barbara Brenner

Forest
by Ron Hirschi

Stringbean's Trip to the Shining Sea
by Vera B. Williams

A Tree Can Be
by Judy Nayer

Where the Forest Meets the Sea
by Jeannie Baker

The Wump World
by Bill Peet

AMERICA THE BEAUTIFUL BULLETIN BOARD

Cut a large cloud, mountain, and wave from butcher paper. Write *We can keep our skies beautiful by . . .* on the cloud, *We can keep our land beautiful by . . .* on the mountain, and *We can keep our water beautiful by . . .* on the wave. Hang each in a classroom corner. Divide the class into three groups and send a group to each shape. Ask groups to finish the sentence on the shape by writing three ideas on it. Have groups rotate and add ideas to each shape. Staple the completed shapes on a bulletin board. Invite students to use art supplies to create a scene around the shapes to highlight their ideas. Add the title *Let's Keep America Beautiful!*

MATERIALS

▲ scissors

▲ white, brown, and blue butcher paper

▲ permanent markers

▲ art supplies (construction paper, crayons or markers, paint and paintbrushes, plastic or paper flowers, raffia or plastic or paper grass, magazine cutouts)

▲ stapler

"SEEING" AIR POLLUTION

Discuss air pollution and its sources and damaging effects. Have students cut springtime shapes (butterflies, flowers, suns, etc.) from plastic milk jugs. Invite students to write their names on the shapes in permanent marker, punch holes, and attach string. Ask students to spread a thin layer of petroleum jelly on one side of the shapes. Have students hang the shapes outside (at least six feet from the ground) in a variety of locations. Leave the strips outside for a week. After collecting them, have students study their shapes. Students will note large particles (probably flying dirt and debris) and changes in the color of the petroleum jelly (signs of pollution). Discuss possible sources for the particles and color changes. Remind students that the particles are in the air we breathe.

IF I WERE A WUMP

Read *The Wump World* aloud. After story discussion, ask students what the Wumps could do after the Pollutions left their planet. Have students brainstorm several solutions. Distribute construction paper to each student. Invite students to write *If I were a Wump, I'd clean up this dump! I'd _____*. Have each student finish the sentence and illustrate it. Compile the pages in a class book titled *If I Were a Wump.*

TRASH-A-THON

MATERIALS
- ▲ writing paper or computer program
- ▲ trash bins

Have students plan and participate in a trash-a-thon in which students take pledges for the pounds of recyclable trash they collect and recycle. For example, a sponsor may pledge one dollar for every fifty pounds of trash recycled. Have students contact local glass, paper, plastic, and aluminum recycling centers for their terms and hours of business. As a class, design a pledge sheet and receipt. Reproduce and distribute the sheets and receipts. Ask students to solicit pledges from family and friends, collect trash on a designated day or week, and turn in the trash for recycling. Ask students to collect their pledges by a specific date and present the donation to a representative from a local environmental group.

MY OWN NATIONAL PARK

MATERIALS
- ▲ national park information (from books, encyclopedias, computer programs, and the Internet)
- ▲ construction paper
- ▲ crayons or markers
- ▲ drawing paper

Explain that the government sets aside land for national parks so that America's wildlife and landscape can be preserved for future generations. Have students learn about the national park system through books, encyclopedias, computer programs, and the Internet. Point out and discuss park accommodations (camping, inns, and cabins) and "natural" park attractions such as geysers, wild animals, and mountains. Invite each student to develop his or her own national park. Ask each student to use construction paper and draw a map that shows the park's attractions and accommodations. Have each student fold drawing paper into thirds and design a pamphlet that includes the park's name, fees, dates of operation, rules, highlighted attractions, and accommodations. Display the maps and pamphlets on a wall under the heading *National Parks—One More Way to Keep America Beautiful!*

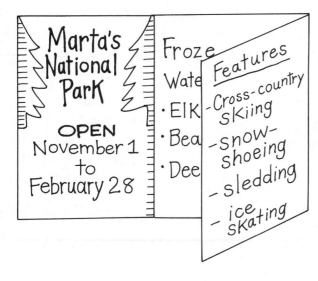

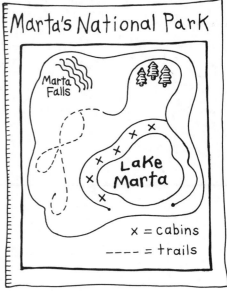

WONDERFUL WATERWAY POSTERS

MATERIALS
▲ poster board
▲ art supplies (paints, paintbrushes, crayons or markers, magazine cutouts, glue)

Plan a trip to a local waterway, such as a river, lake, or ocean. Before the trip, discuss water pollution and ways to eliminate it, such as picking up litter, avoiding the use of gasoline-powered boats, and refraining from dumping chemicals or other liquids in the water. Ask student groups to use poster board and art supplies to design posters that remind visitors to keep the waterway beautiful. Have students obtain permission from a ranger or lifeguard and hang the posters during the trip. Be sure to hang the posters on bulletin boards, trash cans, or other man-made objects so the waterway's natural surroundings are not altered.

BEAUTIFUL AMERICA ALBUM

HOME ACTIVITY

MATERIALS
▲ *Stringbean's Trip to the Shining Sea* by Vera B. Williams
▲ blank photo album pages
▲ photo album

Read *Stringbean's Trip to the Shining Sea* aloud. Have students discuss the beautiful places they have seen in America with their families. Remind students that beautiful places can be out-of-state or in their own backyard. Distribute one blank photo album page to each student. Send letters home asking students and parents to look through family photos and choose two or three that show the beauty of America. Ask families to place the photos or drawings on both sides of the page with a brief explanation of each. Invite families to draw pictures if they do not have photos. Collect the photo album pages and place them in a class album labeled *Beautiful America.*

Beautiful America by Ana

We grow flowers.

Our garden is beautiful.

Beautiful America by Paul

My family thinks Mackinac Island is beautiful.

No cars are allowed on the island.

BUTTERFLIES

Nothing says spring like a flittering, fluttering butterfly! Welcome spring, and the month of April, by studying these miraculous insects. Your students' curiosity will be flying!

BUTTERFLY TREE BULLETIN BOARD

Make a ceiling-to-floor tree trunk and branches by twisting brown butcher paper, and attach the tree to a wall. Tell students that they will demonstrate the life cycle by making caterpillars and chrysalises. Have students make caterpillars by painting four attached egg carton cups. Invite students to add wiggly eyes and stickers or construction-paper decorations. Have students place their caterpillars in paper-towel-tube "chrysalises" and secure them with tape. Tape the chrysalises to the paper tree branches. Explain that within three weeks, the caterpillars will turn into butterflies. Mark the days on the calendar as they pass. Three weeks later, after students have gone home, accordion-fold pieces of tissue paper and gather them in the center to form bow-tie-shaped "butterfly wings." Remove the caterpillars from the chrysalises and tape on the tissue-paper wings so they become butterflies. Tape the butterflies to the tree. The next day, after students see their butterfly tree, read *Let's Find Out About Butterflies* aloud to reinforce the life cycle concept.

MATERIALS
- ▲ brown butcher paper
- ▲ stapler or masking tape
- ▲ paint/paintbrushes
- ▲ egg cartons
- ▲ wiggly eyes
- ▲ stickers or construction-paper scraps
- ▲ glue
- ▲ paper towel tubes
- ▲ tape
- ▲ colored tissue paper
- ▲ *Let's Find Out About Butterflies* by Roy Abish

EDIBLE BUTTERFLIES

Have each student use a craft stick to fill a celery stalk half with cream cheese. Ask students to stick two pretzel twist "wings" in the cream cheese. Have students use pretzel sticks for antennae and add raisin decorations to the cream cheese. Invite students to eat and enjoy their delicious butterflies!

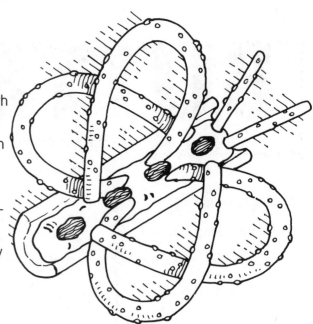

THE VERY HUNGRY BUTTERFLY CLASS BOOK

Read *The Very Hungry Caterpillar* aloud. After story discussion, explain that unlike caterpillars, who eat leaves and fruit, butterflies drink nectar from flowers. Invite each student to cut out flower pictures from a magazine. Have each student cut out only one type of flower such as all roses or tulips. Have students count their flowers and glue them to construction paper. Ask students to design a small construction-paper butterfly and glue it to a flower on the paper. Help students identify the flower types they chose. Assign a day of the week for each student and help him or her write the following sentence frame under the picture: *On (day of the week), the butterfly ate the nectar from (number) (type of flower).* For example, a student might write *On Monday, the butterfly ate the nectar from three daisies.* Compile the pages into a class book titled *The Very Hungry Butterfly.*

On Monday, the butterfly ate the nectar from three daisies.

MATERIALS

▲ butterfly finger puppets (below)

BUTTERFLY POEM

Teach the following poem and motions. Have students practice the poem using their finger puppets and perform it for other classes or parents.

Butterfly, Butterfly	Motions
Butterfly, butterfly, flutter around.	*Students make puppets flutter.*
Butterfly, butterfly, touch the ground.	*Students make puppets land on ground and pop up.*
Butterfly, butterfly, fly so free.	*Students make puppets fly quickly.*
Butterfly, butterfly, land on me!	*Students make puppets land on their noses.*
Butterfly, butterfly, reach the sky.	*Students make puppets fly high.*
Butterfly, butterfly, say *Good-bye!*	*Students make puppets go behind their backs.*

MATERIALS

▲ 4" (10 cm) tissue paper squares
▲ small resealable plastic bags
▲ pencils
▲ whole and half pipe cleaners

BUTTERFLY FINGER PUPPETS

Have students select different-colored tissue paper squares and stuff them into small resealable bags until the bags are full. Have each student "zip" his or her bag, punch a small air hole in the bag with a pencil tip, scrunch it in the middle, and twist a long pipe cleaner around it, folding the ends to make antennae. Ask each student to twist half of a pipe cleaner around the middle and leave a loop so his or her finger can fit through. Have students use their puppets to act out the rhyme above.

MATERIALS

- ▲ 9" x 12" (23 x 31 cm) black construction paper
- ▲ Butterfly Pattern reproducible (page 31)
- ▲ scissors
- ▲ colored tissue paper
- ▲ 3 parts starch and 1 part water mixture
- ▲ 8" x 11" (21.5 x 28 cm) waxed paper pieces
- ▲ glue
- ▲ tape

"STAINED GLASS" BUTTERFLIES

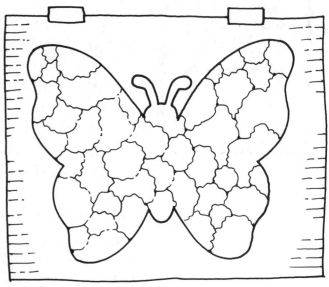

Have each student cut out and trace the Butterfly Pattern reproducible on black construction paper. Ask each student to cut out the butterfly and discard it, keeping the butterfly-shaped border. Ask students to dip torn tissue paper in the starch and water mixture. Have each student place and overlap the tissue paper on a piece of waxed paper until the paper is covered. When dry, have each student glue the waxed paper, tissue side up, in the center of the black construction paper so tissue paper shows through the border. Tape the "stained glass" butterflies to a window so light shines through.

MATERIALS

- ▲ balloons
- ▲ scissors
- ▲ construction paper
- ▲ tape
- ▲ wire hangers
- ▲ pantyhose
- ▲ pliers
- ▲ masking tape or chalk

BUTTERFLY CATCHER

Inflate and close seven balloon "butterflies" (five balloons for the game plus two extra in case some pop). Cut 14 butterfly wings from construction paper and tape two to each balloon. Make five "butterfly nets" by bending five hangers into circles. Pull a pantyhose leg over each circle and tie it in place. With pliers, squeeze the hanger hooks closed. Mark two lines, approximately 10' (3.1 m) across, with masking tape or chalk. Divide the class into five relay teams and give each a butterfly. Have each team line up behind one of the lines. At a signal, have team members toss their butterflies in the air and swat them with the nets from one line to the other and back. If a butterfly hits the ground, the player must return to the first line and begin again. Continue the game until each student has had a turn.

BUTTERFLY SYMMETRY CLASS BOOK

Using individual pieces of construction paper, draw symmetrical half-shapes of a caterpillar, chrysalis, and butterfly that when reflected against a mirror, show whole, realistic images. Draw a dotted line of symmetry next to each image as a guideline for placing a mirror. Label each image. Pass around the drawings and a rectangular mirror. Invite students to use the mirrors, find lines of symmetry, and make reflections of whole images. Leave art supplies in a learning center. Ask students to use the art supplies in their free time to create and hang their own caterpillar, chrysalis, and butterfly half images. Compile the papers in a class book titled *Butterfly Symmetry*. Invite students to read the book and use mirrors to find symmetrical reflections.

ACCORDION CATERPILLARS

Have each student accordion-fold a construction-paper strip ten times to make a paper with twelve flat "faces." Ask each student to unfold the paper and glue a construction-paper circle as a caterpillar head on the first face. Ask students to decorate the head with crayons or markers. Have each student write *C* on the first face of the paper. Ask each student to write *A* on the second face and continue writing letters on faces until they have spelled caterpillar. For each letter, have students think of a food that a caterpillar might eat such as *C—cabbage*, *A—apple*, and *T—tomato*. Invite students to write the words and illustrate them next to their letters. Ask students to staple their caterpillars to construction paper so they pop out. Display the caterpillars on a bulletin board titled *What Do Caterpillars Eat for Lunch?*

AT-HOME BUTTERFLIES

Send a note home asking families to use the Butterfly Pattern reproducible (or their own pattern) and art supplies from home to make the most beautiful butterfly in the world. Explain that the butterflies will be flown in a butterfly parade, and invite the families to attend. Have students return their butterflies on a designated day. Attach strings to dowels and tie the butterflies to the strings. Have students parade through classrooms or on the playground. Hang the butterflies from the ceiling near the title *April Is Blooming with Butterflies!*

BUTTERFLY PATTERN

BICYCLE SAFETY WEEK

When the weather becomes warmer, out come the bikes! Help students use their bikes safely by letting them celebrate Bicycle Safety Week during the third week of April. Students will have fun and learn some "wheelie" good tips!

LITERATURE LINKS

The Bike Lesson
by Stan and Jan Berenstein

Bikes
by Dolores Baugh

Bike Trip
by Betsy Maestro

Curious George Rides a Bike
by H.A. Rey

Little Duck's Bicycle Ride
by Dorothy Stot

The Visual Dictionary of Everyday Things
by Eyewitness Visual Dictionaries

What's the Matter, Sylvie, Can't You Ride?
by Karen Born Anderson

BICYCLE SAFETY BULLETIN BOARD

Discuss bicycle safety by having students brainstorm safety tips such as *Wear a helmet, Ride with the traffic,* and *Obey traffic signals.* Write the tips on the chalkboard. Have students color and cut out bikes from the Bike Pattern reproducibles. Invite students to design a bike flag for their bikes from construction paper. Have students write and illustrate one of the rules listed on the flag. Create an outdoor scene with construction-paper roads and sidewalks on a bulletin board titled *Rules of the Road.* Have students staple their bike patterns and flags on the bulletin board.

MATERIALS
▲ scissors
▲ Bike Pattern reproducible (page 36)
▲ construction paper
▲ crayons or markers
▲ stapler

BICYCLE SAFETY SENTENCE STRIP BOOKS

Have students brainstorm bicycle safety rules. List the rules on chart paper. Have each student write *Bicycle Safety Rule #* on the left side of a whole sentence strip. Ask students to number the half sentence strips one through four and write a bicycle safety rule after each number. Invite students to illustrate the rules. Have students stack the half strips in order and staple them on the right side of the whole strip. Ask students to fold the half strips back and write a fifth rule on the blank part of the whole strip. Invite students to share their books with younger students.

Bicycle Safety Rule # | 1. Follow traffic signals.

THE WHEELS ON THE BIKE

Teach the lyrics and motions to "The Wheels on the Bike." Have students practice and perform the song for parents or other classes.

The Wheels on the Bike
(to the tune of "The Wheels on the Bus")

	Motions
The wheels on the bike go round and round, round and round, round and round. The wheels on the bike go round and round, all through the town.	*Students spin paper plates like steering wheels.*
The helmet for the bike goes on my head, on my head, on my head. The helmet for the bike goes on my head, all through the town.	*Students place hats on their heads.*
The reflector on my bike says, *Here I come, Here I come, Here I come.* The reflector on my bike says, *Here I come,* all through the town.	*Students wave mirrors left to right.*
The bell on my bike says, *Watch out now, Watch out now, Watch out now.* The bell on my bike says, *Watch out now,* all through the town.	*Students ring bells.*

OBSTACLE COURSE

Set up an outdoor obstacle course on blacktop with "start" and "finish" chalk lines, pylons through which to weave, traffic-signal posters (showing red or green circles), and dotted and solid chalk lines for a divided "road." Take students outside to the course. Explain how to complete the course correctly through the use of bicycle safety rules. Have students complete the course on scooter boards, pretending the boards are bikes. Invite each student to complete the course at least once. For extra fun, invite students to rearrange and design their own course before riding again.

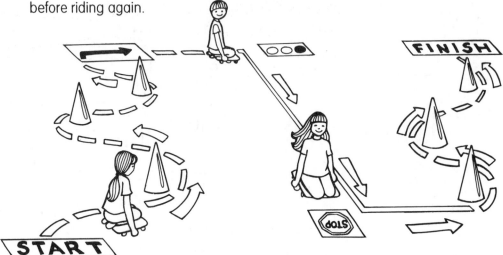

BIKES THROUGH HISTORY BOOK

Share pages 58 and 59 of *The Visual Dictionary of Everyday Things,* which give a short history of the bicycle and show labeled photographs of mountain bike parts. Explain that the bicycle has changed throughout history and the mountain bike is one modern version. Divide the class into groups of three led by an older student or adult volunteer. Ask each group to research one type of bicycle. Have students illustrate the bicycle on one side of a piece of construction paper and write *Do you know about this bicycle?* under the illustration. Have each group prepare a fact sheet about the bicycle on writing paper and glue it on the back of the illustration. Invite groups to share their pages. Have the class sequence the bikes chronologically and bind the pages in a class book titled *Bikes Through History.*

HAND SIGNAL JIVE

Teach the following chant and motions to reinforce correct hand signals for bicycle riding. Invite students to perform the chant for parents or other classes.

Hand Signal Jive

I hold my left arm out
(*Students hold left arm out.*)
when I want to turn left.
(*Students hold left arm out.*)
That's the hand signal jive
(*Students clap in rhythm.*)
and there are two more signals left.

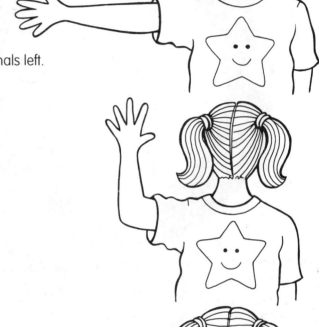

I bend my left arm up
(*Students bend left arm up.*)
when I want to turn right.
(*Students bend left arm up.*)
That's the hand signal jive
(*Students clap in rhythm.*)
and it's really out of sight.

I bend my left arm down
(*Students bend left arm down.*)
when I want to make a stop.
(*Students bend left arm down.*)
That's the hand signal jive
(*Students clap in rhythm.*)
and it keeps me tip-top.

(Repeat verse one.)

FAMILY RULE T-SHIRTS

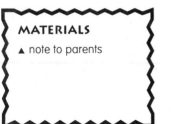

Send a note home asking students and family members to think of a bicycle rule (it does not have to be a safety rule) they have for their family such as *Never leave your bike in the driveway, Always wear your helmet* or *Always lock up your bike.* Ask each family to design a T-shirt stating and illustrating the rule. Invite families to use fabric paints, embroidery, appliqué, permanent markers, or any other medium to design their shirts. Invite students to wear and share their shirts on the last day of Bicycle Safety Week.

BIKE PATTERN

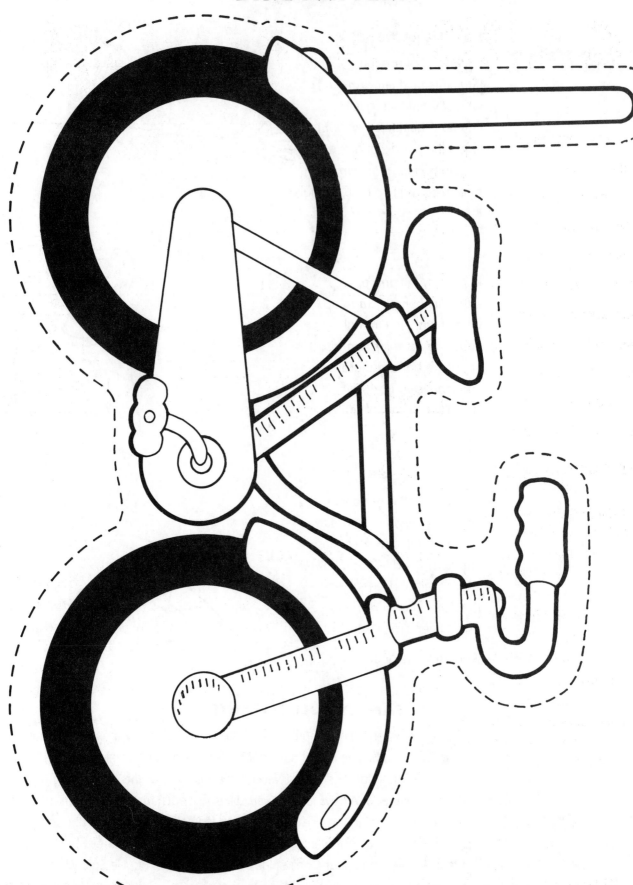

Bicycle Safety Week

NATIONAL GARDEN MONTH

Make sure this April is blooming with trees, shrubs, flowers, and excitement by celebrating National Garden Month with your students. Your students will learn important science concepts as well as have fun. So start gardening in the classroom today—it's a growing experience for everyone!

LITERATURE LINKS

A Child's Garden of Verses
by Robert Louis Stevenson

The Carrot Seed
by Ruth Krauss

Falling Up
by Shel Silverstein

A Garden Alphabet
by Isabel Wilner

Growing Vegetable Soup
by Lois Ehlert

Linnea in Monet's Garden
by Christina Bjork

The Magic School Bus Plants Seeds
by Joanna Cole

Planting a Rainbow
by Lois Ehlert

We Can Eat Plants,
CTP Learn to Read Series

SELECT A SEED BULLETIN BOARD

Gather a variety of seeds such as orange seeds, avocado or cherry pits, beans, apple seeds, sunflower seeds, garlic, grape seeds, or popcorn. Glue each seed type to a separate index card. Number the seed cards and hang them on a bulletin board titled *Select a Seed and Make a Match!* Next to each seed card, attach an empty library pocket. At the bottom of the board, hang a library pocket labeled *Seed Names*. Write the name of each seed on an index card and place the cards in the *Seed Names* pocket. Create an answer key by writing each seed name and its matching number on writing paper and placing the paper in a folder. Invite students to come to the board, read the seed names, and try to make matches by placing name cards in the correct seeds' library pockets. Have students self-check by consulting the answer key.

MATERIALS
▲ variety of seeds
▲ glue
▲ index cards
▲ library pockets
▲ writing paper
▲ folder

THE GARDENER

Read aloud "The Gardener," a poem that shares a child's view of a hard-working gardener who will not come out to play. Discuss the situation from the child's point of view (the child wonders why the gardener works during nice weather instead of playing). Then have students brainstorm the gardener's possible reasons for working instead of playing, such as gardening is his job or gardening is fun and he would rather garden than play. Have students fold construction paper in half. Have students imagine they are the child and on the left side finish the sentence *I think you should play because* _____. Have students imagine they are the gardener and on the right side finish the sentence *I will garden because* _____. Have students illustrate their sentences. Copy "The Gardener" on chart paper and display it on a bulletin board. Hang the illustrations around the poem. Attach the title *Play or Garden? Garden or Play? What Would You Do On This Fine Day?*

A GARDEN OF GROWING CHILDREN

Invite students to glue photocopies of their class photos to construction-paper circles as flower centers. Demonstrate how to cut round, pointed, and scalloped flower petals from construction paper. Have students cut their own petals and glue them to the circle backs. Ask each student to glue his or her flower to a craft stick. Have students cut leaves from green construction paper and glue them to the craft stick sides. Ask each student to place crumpled green tissue paper in a baby food jar and push the craft sticks into the jar. Display the "potted flowers" on a table covered with plastic or paper grass. Add the title *A Garden of Growing Children is a Beauty to Behold.*

VEGETABLE SOUP CLASS BOOK

MATERIALS

▲ *Growing Vegetable Soup* by Lois Ehlert
▲ chart paper
▲ construction paper
▲ crayons or markers
▲ scissors
▲ glue
▲ bookbinding materials
▲ plastic bowl and spoon

Read *Growing Vegetable Soup* aloud. After story discussion, invite students to brainstorm vegetable names (at least one for each student in class). Record the list on chart paper. Ask each student to design a different vegetable using construction paper, crayons or markers, and scissors. Have students glue their vegetable cutouts to construction paper. Help students complete the following sentence frame: *(Student name) put in a (vegetable name)*. For example, a student might write under their cutouts *Sarah put in a carrot*. Design a class book cover from construction paper. Glue a construction-paper cooking pot to the cover. Write *Class Vegetable Soup* on the pot. On the inside front cover, write *Our class made vegetable soup. Everyone added a vegetable.* Bind student papers in the book. Draw a bowl and spoon on the inside back cover, and write in the bowl *Our class put in a spoon and ate it all up! Yum!*

MY GARDEN FINGERPLAY

MATERIALS

▲ none

Teach the following fingerplay and accompanying motions. Have students practice and perform the fingerplay for parents or other classes.

My Garden	**Motions**
This is my garden. I'll rake it with care.	*Students extend one hand forward and make a raking motion on palm with fingers of other hand.*
Here are the flower seeds I'll plant in there.	*Students make planting motion with thumb and index finger.*
The sun will shine and the rain will fall.	*Students make a circle overhead with hands and then let fingers flutter down.*
And my garden will blossom and grow straight and tall.	*Students cup hands together and extend slowly upward.*

National Garden Month

MATERIALS

▲ "My Nose Garden" by Shel Silverstein (from *Falling Up*)
▲ magazines
▲ scissors
▲ construction paper
▲ glue
▲ chart paper

MY NOSE GARDEN

Read "My Nose Garden" aloud. Invite students to brainstorm other body parts that might be fun to grow in a garden, such as hands, ears, or hair. Ask each student to choose one body part, find pictures of it in magazines, and cut the pictures out. Have students draw body-part gardens on construction paper and glue the magazine pictures to the plants. Copy "My Nose Garden" on chart paper and display it on a bulletin board surrounded by student body-part gardens. Add the title *What Do You Know . . . Our Body Parts Grow!*

MATERIALS

▲ sponges
▲ tempera paints/paintbrushes
▲ white butcher paper
▲ scissors
▲ stapler
▲ newspaper
▲ glue
▲ paper grocery sacks
▲ butcher paper
▲ markers

GIANT FRUITS AND VEGETABLES

Invite each student to sponge-paint three large pieces of white butcher paper, each a different color. When dry, have students fold one paper in half, draw a fruit or vegetable on it, and cut it out to make two identical shapes. Have students repeat with the other two pieces of paper. Ask students to join the two matching pieces of each fruit or vegetable, and staple the pieces three-quarters of the way around. Ask students to stuff the shapes with newspaper and staple closed. Invite students to glue on construction-paper leaves or stems. Ask each student to roll the top of a paper grocery sack down so it resembles a basket. Have students staple twisted butcher paper handles to the baskets and place their fruits and vegetables inside. Help each student write the following sentence frame on the front of the basket: *(Student's name, Student's name), how does your garden grow? With (fruit or vegetable), (fruit or vegetable), and (fruit or vegetable) all in a row!*

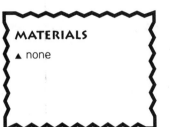
THE FARMER PLANTS THE SEEDS

Teach the following song and motions. Have students practice and perform the song for parents or other classes.

The Farmer Plants the Seeds (to the tune of "The Farmer in the Dell")	**Motions**
The farmer plants the seeds. The farmer plants the seeds. Hi, Ho, the dairy-oh. The farmer plants the seeds.	*Students make planting motion with thumb and index finger.*
(Verse 2) The sun comes out to shine.	*Students make a circle overhead with hands, swaying arms left and right.*
(Verse 3) The rain begins to fall.	*Students' fingers flutter down.*
(Verse 4) The seeds begin to grow.	*Students' hands come together and shoot upward.*
(Verse 5) The farmer digs up food.	*Students make shoveling motion.*
(Verse 6) Now we get to eat.	*Students bring imaginary spoon to mouth.*

MATERIALS

▲ garden journal (blank book of drawing paper)
▲ Seed Sack reproducible (page 42)
▲ book about seeds (such as *We Can Eat Plants* by Rozanne Lanczak Williams, *Planting a Rainbow* by Lois Ehlert, or *The Carrot Seed* by Ruth Krauss)
▲ paper cups
▲ resealable plastic bags filled with soil
▲ vegetable seed packets
▲ potting soil
▲ burlap sack

SEED SACK

HOME ACTIVITY

Place a garden journal, Seed Sack reproducible, book about seeds, paper cup, plastic bag filled with soil, and three or four seed packets in a burlap sack. Label the sack *Seed Sack*. Send the burlap sack and Seed Sack reproducible home with a student, asking him or her to return it the next day. Replenish the sack each morning and send the sack home with a different student each afternoon. Once a week, invite students to give a progress report.

SEED SACK

Date _____

Dear Family,

April is National Garden Month. To celebrate, I'd like you to plant some seeds with me! Please follow the directions below and then return this sack to school tomorrow so my friends can plant seeds, too.

1. Read the enclosed book with me.

2. Choose four or five seeds from a packet and plant them in the cup with soil.

3. Place the cup by a window and water the seeds so the soil stays moist.

4. In the garden journal, help me illustrate the plant that will grow from the seeds. Help me label the parts I can eat.

5. Return the sack, journal, and seed packets to school.

APRIL FOOL'S DAY

April 1

Pranksters beware—this is the day that the joke may be on you! April Fool's Day is a tradition believed to have begun in France. In the mid-1560s, the king of France changed New Year's Day from April 1 to January 1. People who continued to celebrate New Year's Day in April were called "April fools." Your students will have a terrific time with the following April Fool's Day activities—no foolin'!

LITERATURE LINKS

April Fool
by Mary Blount Christian

April Fool's Day
by Emily Kelley

Arthur's April Fool
by Marc Brown

Look Out, It's April Fool's Day
by Frank Modell

FRONT

Here is a little bear
Who is really quite funny.
When you turn him over,
He's an April Fool's Bunny!

BACK

APRIL FOOL'S DAY BEAR/BUNNY

Cut out the Bear/Bunny Pattern and trace it on tagboard to make several patterns. Have students trace a pattern onto construction paper and cut it out. Have students use crayons or markers to draw and color a bear's face. Ask students to turn the paper over and upside-down. Invite students to tell what other animal shape they see (a bunny). Ask students to draw and color a bunny face between the bunny ears (bear legs). Help students read and write the following poem on the bear belly: *Here is a little bear who is really quite funny. When you turn him over, he's an April Fool's bunny!* Hang the bears with tacks so observers can find the bunnies.

MATERIALS

▲ Bear/Bunny Pattern reproducible (page 45)
▲ scissors
▲ tagboard
▲ construction paper
▲ crayons or markers

SWITCHEROO

Fool students with a teacher-switch day. In advance, have the staff draw names to determine where each teacher will spend his or her day. Have each teacher write lesson plans for his or her teacher-switch substitute. On April Fool's Day, make the switch and teach for each other. Both teachers and students will have a great time and will gain greater appreciation for each other.

POISSON D'AVRIL

In France, people who are tricked on April Fool's Day are called *Poisson d'Avril* (April fish). They are given this name because fish born in spring are easily fooled by a baited hook and caught. In the morning, play a French April Fool's Day game by having each student draw and cut out five brightly colored fish. Ask students to write their names on the fish. Have students place a piece of masking tape on each fish. In the afternoon, challenge students to tape the fish on "unsuspecting victims" without getting caught.

BEAR/BUNNY PATTERN

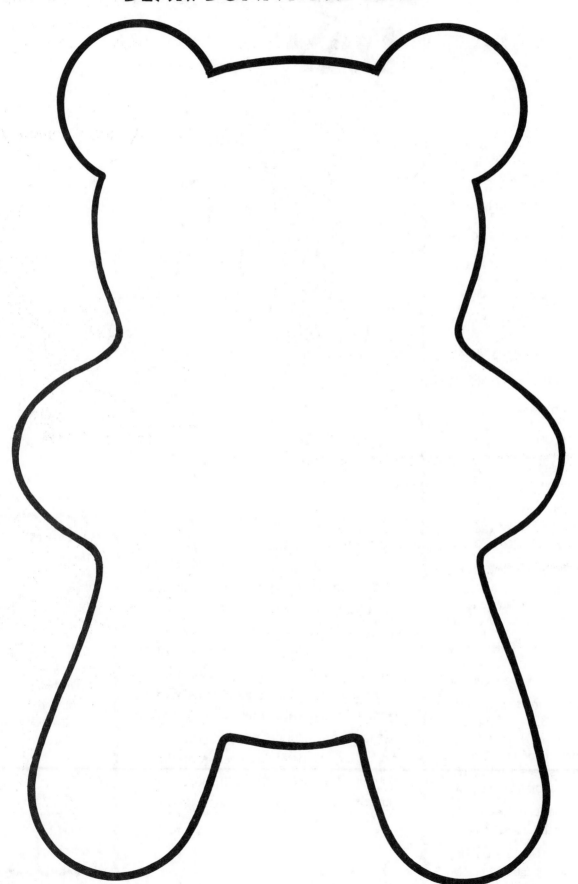

UGLY DUCKLING DAY

April 2

A true artist, Hans Christian Andersen not only wrote poignant, timeless stories, he also made intricate cut-paper designs. Andersen wrote 156 fairy tales and is Denmark's most famous author. So celebrate Andersen's birthday with the following activities—they are fairy-tale fun for everyone!

LITERATURE LINKS

The Emperor's New Clothes
by Hans Christian Andersen
(retold and illustrated by
Nadine Bernard Westcott)

The Emperor Penguin's New Clothes
by Janet Perlman

Eric Carle's Treasure of Classic Stories for Children
by Aesop, Hans Christian Andersen, and the Brothers Grimm (selected, retold, and illustrated by Eric Carle)

The Principal's New Clothes
by Stephanie Calmenson

The Ugly Duckling
by Hans Christian Andersen

TAILOR-MADE PENGUINS

Read aloud and compare *The Emperor's New Clothes* and *The Emperor Penguin's New Clothes*. Have each student design and cut out a penguin body from black construction paper and a bib from white construction paper. Invite students to cut orange construction paper to make beaks, and glue the beaks and bibs on the bodies. Have students draw eyes with white crayons. Have students use fabric or wallpaper scraps to design new clothes for their penguins. Encourage students to be creative—they can consult story illustrations or fashion magazines for ideas.

MATERIALS
▲ *The Emperor's New Clothes* by Hans Christian Andersen (retold and illustrated by Nadine Bernard Westcott)

▲ *The Emperor Penguin's New Clothes* by Janet Perlman

▲ black, white, and orange construction paper

▲ scissors

▲ glue

▲ white crayons

▲ fabric or wallpaper scraps

▲ fashion magazines

MATERIALS

▲ any Hans Christian Andersen story

▲ drawing paper

CHARACTER CONTINUUM

Read aloud a Hans Christian Andersen story such as *The Princess and the Pea,* *The Ugly Duckling,* *The Emperor's New Clothes,* *The Nightingale,* *Thumbelina,* *The Little Match Girl,* *The Little Mermaid,* *The Snow Queen,* *The Red Shoes,* or *The Fir Tree.* Have the class name the story's main characters. Distribute drawing paper to each student. Have students draw a horizontal line across their paper. Ask students to write *good* on the left end of the line and *bad* on the right. Ask students to think about each character, decide if he or she is good or bad, and place the character's name on the line to show how good or bad he or she is. Form student pairs. Ask students to share their continuums with their partners and justify their answers by citing events from the story.

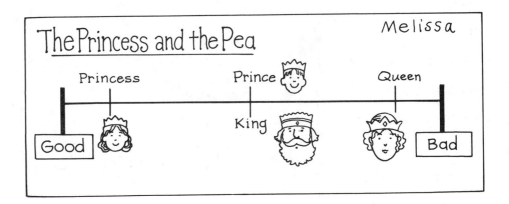

MATERIALS

▲ art supplies (butcher, construction, and tissue paper; crayons or markers; glue; plastic or paper grass; plastic or paper flowers)

▲ *The Ugly Duckling* by Hans Christian Andersen

▲ Signet and Swan reproducible (page 48)

▲ pushpins

FROM SIGNETS TO SWANS

Have students work together and use art supplies to create a pond scene from *The Ugly Ducking.* Display the scene on a bulletin board. Invite each student to decorate a signet and swan from the reproducible. Have students pin their signets on the scene's ground or pond. Invite students to read a specific number of books within a three-week period. Each time a student finishes a book, he or she writes the book name on the signet. When students read the designated number of books, invite them to "become swans" by removing the signets and pinning swans in the sky. After students attach swans, have them make new signets. Challenge the class to fill the sky with swans.

SIGNET AND SWAN

FLY A KITE DAY

April 4

On April 4, 1976, the most kites on a single string were flown in Japan, setting a new world record. The single kite string flew 1,050 kites nearly 4,000 feet in the air! Welcome April's breezes by celebrating Fly a Kite Day—your students' spirits will soar!

LITERATURE LINKS

The Big Kite Contest
by Dorotha Ruthstrom

A Carp for Kimiko
by Virginia Kroll

Curious George Flies a Kite
by Margaret Rey

The Dragon Kite
by Nancy Luenn

Kite Flying Is for Me
by Tom Moran

CLASSROOM KITE FLYING

Have students make simple kites by taping yarn strands to diamond-shaped cutouts and tying cloth strips to the yarn. Teach students the song and motions to "My Kite." Have students perform the song for parents or other classes.

MATERIALS
▲ tape
▲ yarn strands
▲ diamond-shaped construction-paper cutouts
▲ cloth strips

My Kite
(to the tune of "The Farmer in the Dell")

My kite is going high.
My kite is going high.
Oh my, just watch it fly.
My kite is going high.

My kite is falling down.
My kite is falling down.
Oh no, it's down so low.
My kite is falling down.

The wind has caught my kite.
The wind has caught my kite.
What fun, I'm on the run.
The wind has caught my kite.

Motions

Students place kite on toe.
Students place kite on knee.
Students place kite on shoulder.
Students place kite overhead.

Students place kite on shoulder.
Students place kite on knee.
Students place kite on toe.
Students place kite on floor.

Students hold yarn and jog with kite.

MATERIALS

▲ tagboard

▲ scissors

▲ *A Carp for Kimiko* by Virginia Kroll

▲ 12" x 18" (31 cm x 46 cm) light-colored construction paper

▲ crayons or markers

▲ glue

▲ hole punch

▲ 24" (62 cm) yarn strands

FLYING HIGH

Draw a fish shape on several pieces of tagboard and cut the shapes out to make tracing templates. Read *A Carp for Kimiko* aloud. After story discussion, have each student fold construction paper in half and place the mouth of a fish template along the fold. Have students trace around the rest of the body. Ask students to cut along the tracing line, being careful not to cut the fold apart. Have students decorate and color both sides of their fish. Invite each student to glue the long sides of the fish together, leaving the tail open. Punch holes in the mouths and tie on yarn strands. Hang the fish kites from the ceiling to fill the "sky" with flying fish.

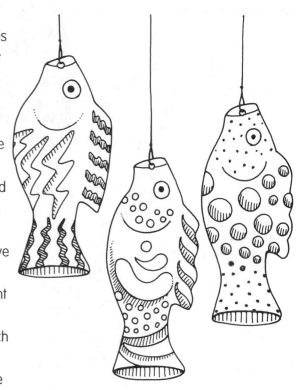

MATERIALS

▲ Robin Kite Pattern reproducible (page 51)

▲ crayons or markers

▲ scissors

▲ tape

▲ drinking straws

▲ hole punch

▲ paper ribbon

▲ string

RED ROBIN KITE

Have students brainstorm springtime items such as sunshine, warm breezes, or flowers. Have each student draw two springtime items on a Robin Kite Pattern. Ask each student to cut out the pattern, fold the robin down the center, and staple just above the fold along the robin's body. Have each student bend the robin's wings down and out (so the robin resembles an air-plane) and staple a drink-ing straw across its back. Invite students to add streamers to the tail by punching holes in the tails and adding paper ribbon. Have students punch a hole in the robin's eye and tie a long "kite string" to it. Take students to the play-ground and invite them to welcome April and the robins by flying their springtime kites.

ROBIN KITE

EASTER

The first Sunday after the first full moon following the first day of spring is Easter. Easter is the day Christians celebrate the resurrection of Jesus Christ. Easter symbols include bunnies, eggs, and all things spring. Have your students learn about Easter and its symbols with the following activities.

LITERATURE LINKS

April Rabbits
by David Cleveland

The Big Bunny and the Easter Eggs
by Steven Kroll

The Little Rabbit
by Judy Dunn

Little Rabbit's Loose Tooth
by Lucy Bates

The Runaway Bunny
by Margaret Wise Brown

Seven Eggs
by Meredith Hooper

Tap! Tap! . . . The Egg Cracked
by Keith Faulkner

3-D EASTER CARDS

Ask students to cut two large ovals from construction paper. Have students press down hard with crayons and color one oval to represent an Easter egg. Invite students to paint the egg with the "wash." When dry, ask each student to poke a hole in the middle of his or her egg, cut four or five slits away from the hole, and fold the slits back. Have students glue the remaining oval, along the edge, behind the colored egg. Ask students to write a short Easter message in the window created by the flaps on the colored egg. Invite students to glue a fuzzy yellow chick next to their message so the chick is popping out of the egg. Send the cards home.

MATERIALS
▲ water
▲ blue or green water "wash" (one cup water mixed with one table-spoon blue or green tempera paint)
▲ scissors
▲ construction paper
▲ crayons
▲ paintbrushes
▲ glue
▲ fuzzy yellow chicks (available at craft stores)

HAIRY EGGS

MATERIALS

▲ 2–3 dozen eggs
▲ 1" x 4" (2.5 cm x 10 cm) tagboard strips
▲ tape
▲ fine-tipped markers
▲ soil
▲ grass seed
▲ water

Eggs have become a common Easter symbol because a hatching egg is symbolic of Jesus Christ emerging from the tomb. Carefully crack eggs so the shell halves resemble jagged cups. Rinse the shells and set aside. Have students bend tagboard strips into circles and tape ends together to create an egg base. Have each student draw a silly face with fine-tipped markers on an egg half and place it on the base. Ask students to fill their shells with soil. Have students plant grass seed in the shells and add water. Place the shells near a window. Within two weeks, students will have hairy eggs. (If students continue to water the grass, they can give their eggs haircuts!)

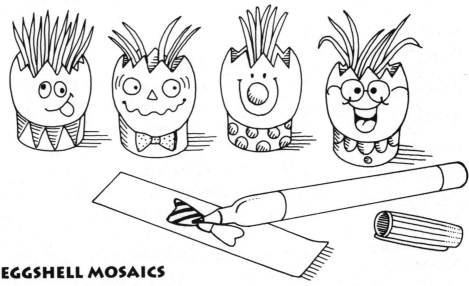

EGGSHELL MOSAICS

MATERIALS

▲ colored eggshells
▲ resealable plastic bags
▲ crayons or markers
▲ pastel-colored construction paper
▲ glue

Invite students to separate colored eggshells into color categories and bring them to class. Have students place like-colored shells in resealable plastic bags and crush them with their fists. Ask students to draw springtime scenes on construction paper. Invite students to fill in the pictures with glue and sprinkle crushed shells over the glue to turn their pictures into colorful mosaics.

CHUBBY BUNNY

Bunnies are a popular Easter symbol and probably became associated with Easter because the hare is a symbol for the moon. The moon is used to determine the date of Easter. Invite students to enjoy this bunny activity together. Have students sit in a circle. Place three marshmallows in front of each student. One at a time, invite students to put two or three marshmallows in their mouths and say *Chubby Bunny* after each goes in. Have the rest of the class count each marshmallow as it goes in. (Invite students to empty the marshmallows into napkins instead of swallowing.) The student who can say *Chubby Bunny* most clearly while holding the marshmallows in his or her mouth wins the "chubby bunny" award—a bag of marshmallows.

BUNNY BONNETS

MATERIALS
▲ sturdy paper bowls
▲ 10" (25.5 cm) paper plates
▲ scissors
▲ glue
▲ stapler
▲ ribbon
▲ tempera paint/paintbrushes
▲ hat-decorating supplies (construction paper, crayons, tape, cotton balls)

Have each student turn a paper bowl rim-side-down in the center of an upside-down paper plate and trace around it. Ask each student to cut a circle from the plate's middle (staying slightly inside the tracing line) to create a ring. Have each student glue the bowl rim to the inner edge of the ring to make a brimmed bonnet. Ask students to staple ribbons on both sides of their bonnets to create ties. Invite students to paint the bonnets. When dry, have students cut bunny ears from construction paper and color the centers to match their bonnets' colors. Have students cut two 1/2" (1 cm) slits in the top of their bonnets and push the ear bottoms through. Ask students to turn their bonnets over and tape the ear bottoms in place on the inside. Have each student glue a cotton-ball "tail" to the back of his or her bonnet. Invite students to wear the bonnets and sing "Did You Ever See a Bunny?" (page 55).

DID YOU EVER SEE A BUNNY?

Have students wear their bunny bonnets (page 54) and place colored dot stickers on their noses. Teach the following song and motions. Have students perform the song for parents or other classes.

Did You Ever See a Bunny?
(to the tune of "Did You Ever See a Lassie?")

Motions

Did you ever see a bunny, a bunny, a bunny,
Did you ever see a bunny munching his lunch?
He munches and crunches,
and munches and crunches.
Did you ever see a bunny munching his lunch?

Students munch carrots.

Did you ever see a bunny, a bunny, a bunny,
Did you ever see a bunny wiggle his nose?
He wiggles and giggles,
and wiggles and giggles.
Did you ever see a bunny wiggle his nose?

Students wiggle noses.

Did you ever see a bunny, a bunny, a bunny,
Did you ever see a bunny flap his big ears?
He flips them and flaps them,
and flips them and flaps them.
Did you ever see a bunny flap his big ears?

Students shake head.

Did you ever see a bunny, a bunny, a bunny,
Did you ever see a bunny hop down the street?
He hips and he hops,
and he hips and he hops.
Did you ever see a bunny hop down the street?

Students hop in place.

LIBRARY DAY

On April 9, 1833, the first free public library in the United States opened in Petersboro, New Hampshire. Share the love of the library and books by celebrating National Library Day. The following activities show you how!

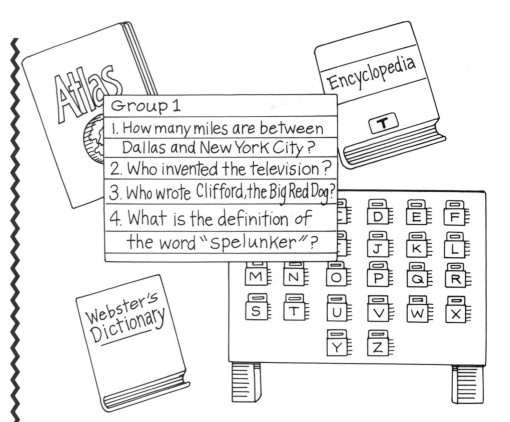

Group 1
1. How many miles are between Dallas and New York City?
2. Who invented the television?
3. Who wrote Clifford, the Big Red Dog?
4. What is the definition of the word "spelunker"?

LITERATURE LINKS

Aunt Lulu
by Daniel Pinkwater

Check It Out: The Book about Libraries
by Gail Gibbons

Goliath's Birthday
by Terrence Dicks

How a Book Is Made
by Aliki

How My Library Grew by Dinah
by Martha G. Alexander

I Like the Library
by Ann Rockwell

I Want to Be a Librarian
by Donna Baker

Miss Rumphius
by Barbara Cooney

LIBRARY SCAVENGER HUNT

Plan a field trip to the public or school library. Prepare five question cards (index cards) with four different questions on each. Write one question whose answer can be found in an atlas, one whose answer can be found in an encyclopedia, one whose answer can be found in a card catalog/computer, and one whose answer can be found in a dictionary. On the day of the trip, divide the class into five groups, each with an adult chaperone. After the library tour, distribute question cards and invite groups to find the answers. Have chaperones record the answers on the cards' backs. Back in class, share the questions, answers, and materials used to find the answers.

MATERIALS
▲ index cards
▲ library reference materials (atlases, encyclopedias, card catalogs/computers, dictionaries)

BOOK EXCHANGE

One week prior to National Library Day, send home a note asking parents to allow their child to donate a used children's book in exchange for another. On National Library Day, place all donated books on a table. Invite students to silently review the books and choose one to keep. After book selection, invite students to read and share their "new" books.

BEAUTIFUL-PLACE CLASS BOOK

Read aloud *Miss Rumphius*, the story of a librarian who wanted to make the world a more beautiful place. Have students brainstorm one thing they can do to make the world a more beautiful place. Invite each student to fold a half piece of drawing paper in half and write his or her idea on the left side. Have students illustrate their ideas on the right. Ask students to fold a piece of 6" x 9" (15 cm x 23 cm) construction paper in half to make a cover for their "books." Invite each student to glue the writing/illustration inside the cover. Have each student decorate the cover and title the book *I Can Make the World a Beautiful Place*. Have each student glue the back of the cover to a piece of construction paper and write his or her name at the top. Bind the papers in a class book.

PET DAY

April 10

On April 10, 1866, the ASPCA (Association for the Protection Against Cruelty to Animals) was founded. To highlight the love and respect people should have for animals, celebrate Pet Day with your class. The following activities are, as a pet kitty would say, "purrfect."

LITERATURE LINKS

Can I Keep Him?
by Steven Kellogg

Goliath's Birthday
by Terrence Dicks

Have You Seen My Cat?
by Eric Carle

Pet Animals
by Lucy Cousins

Pets
by Claire Watts

Positively No Pets Allowed
by Nathan Zimelman

Rosalie
by Joan Hewett

Will You Please Feed Our Cat?
by James Stevenson

PAPER PET PARADE

Have students each paint a picture of their favorite pet on white construction paper. When dry, have students trace on another piece of paper and cut out their pet shapes to create a backing. Have students stack the papers and staple three-fourths of the way around. Ask students to stuff the shapes with newspaper and staple closed. Have students place their "pets" on the floor. As a class, sort and group the pets by species, color, and size in "real life". Have students arrange the pets from smallest to largest. After each pet is placed in line, have the student who made it explain why it his or her favorite. Have students attach string to the pets and hang them in "size order" from the ceiling. At the front of the line, hang the title *Paper Pets on Parade.*

MATERIALS

▲ tempera paints/paint-brushes
▲ white construction paper
▲ scissors
▲ newspaper
▲ stapler
▲ string

MATERIALS

▲ *Goliath's Birthday* by Terrence Dicks

▲ 12" (31 cm) diameter construction-paper circles

▲ crayons or markers

▲ scissors

▲ tape

▲ stapler

▲ yarn

▲ animal-shaped cookies

PET BIRTHDAY PARTY

Read *Goliath's Birthday* aloud. After story discussion, have students each decorate a paper circle to celebrate their pets' birthdays or birthdays of pets they'd like to own. Have each student cut a slit from the edge of the circle to the center and fold it into a cone-shaped birthday hat. Ask each student to tape the cone together and staple yarn to both sides for ties. To have a pet birthday party, have students wear the hats, eat animal-shaped cookies with their mouths only (no hands allowed), and sing "Happy Pet Day to You" to the tune of "Happy Birthday."

MATERIALS

▲ none

E-I-E-I-O

Discuss pets and the sounds they make. Invite each student to name a pet they would like to have and imitate its sound. Have students use their pet ideas and sounds in a variation of "Old MacDonald Had a Farm." Ask the class to go from student to student and sing the following song lyrics.

(student's name) has a super pet.
E-I-E-I-O
Her/His pet is a (type of pet).
E-I-E-I-O

With a (pet sound, pet sound) here,
And a (pet sound, pet sound) there.
Here a (pet sound), there a (pet sound).
Everywhere a (pet sound, pet sound).

(student's name) has a super pet.
E-I-E-I-O

PASSOVER

Fifteenth day of the Hebrew month of Nisan

Passover, the Jewish festival of freedom, lasts for eight days. Passover is celebrated with several traditions, including a feast and ceremony called the Seder. Help your students become familiar with one aspect of Jewish culture by learning about Passover—their interest in all cultures will grow.

LITERATURE LINKS

Good-Bye House
by Frank Asch

Matzoh Ball Fairy
by Carla Heymsfeld

Passover
by June Behrens

The Passover Parrot
by Evelyn Zusman

A Picture Book of Passover
by David A. Adler

Sammy Spider's First Passover
by Sylvia A. Rouss

PASSOVER STORY

Teach students the following words by introducing motions: *flee* (hands slap lap to make running sound), *dough* (hands knead imaginary dough), *desert* (hands wipe forehead as if it is hot), and *Red Sea* (hands move in a wave motion). Read the following story to the class. Whenever you say a word with an accompanying motion, have students perform the motion. If you wish, read the story faster a second time and challenge students to motion more quickly.

Passover Story

Passover celebrates the story of the Israelites who were once slaves in Egypt. God punished the Egyptians with 10 plagues for keeping the slaves, but passed over the Israelites and did not punish them. The Israelites were finally freed by the Egyptians and had to **flee** quickly. Because they had to **flee**, there wasn't time to bake **dough** for bread. They stored **dough** without yeast to take with them. As they crossed the **desert**, they baked the **dough** in the hot sun and made crackers called matzohs. The Israelites came to the **Red Sea**, their path through the **desert**. A miracle happened—the **Red Sea** parted and the Israelites could cross and **flee** to freedom.

MATERIALS
▲ none

SEDER SYMBOLS

Place each food symbol on four plates. Set aside. Discuss popular symbols such as a triangle with arrows (symbolizes recycling) or a clover (symbolizes good luck). Explain that during Passover Jewish people display and eat special foods during a meal called the *Seder* to symbolize Passover's meaning. Divide the class into four groups. Distribute a reproducible to each group and read aloud numbers one through six, the sentences that tell the meaning behind each food symbol. Distribute a food plate to each group. Have groups cut out sentences one through six from the reproducible and place each next to the food they think it represents. When complete, share the correct answers (below) and discuss how each food symbolizes what is explained in each sentence.

Symbol Explanation	Food/Symbol
1. This is a symbol of the bitterness the Jewish people felt when they were slaves in Egypt.	bitter herbs
2. This is a symbol of the mortar the Jewish slaves used to make bricks in Egypt.	charoses
3. This is a symbol of God's outstretched arm, helping the Jewish people when they are in trouble.	shank bone
4. This is a symbol of the cycle of life.	boiled egg
5. This is a symbol of spring and its promise of hope. It also symbolizes Jewish people's faith in the future.	parsley
6. This is a symbol of the tears cried by the Israelite slaves.	salt water

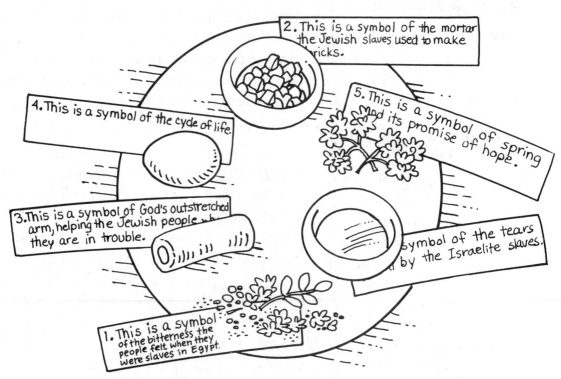

WHAT WOULD YOU TAKE?

MATERIALS

▲ *Good-Bye House* by Frank Asch
▲ crayons or markers
▲ construction paper
▲ bookbinding materials

Read *Good-Bye House* aloud. After story discussion, ask students what they would take if they had to move, like the Israelites did. Have students draw their ideas on construction paper. During drawing time, help each student write and complete the sentence *If I had to move, I would take _____* on the construction paper. Bind the papers in a class book titled *If I Had to Move . . . .*

MATZOH BREI

MATERIALS

▲ mixing bowls and spoons
▲ 6 matzohs
▲ 2–4 cups water (for soaking)
▲ 4 eggs
▲ 4 tablespoons milk
▲ dash of salt
▲ 4 tablespoons margarine
▲ electric skillet
▲ plates, forks, and napkins

Matzoh symbolizes the unleavened bread the Israelites ate as they crossed the desert to freedom. To remember this, Jewish people sometimes eat matzoh brei for breakfast during Passover. Explain matzoh's significance and then make and share the following recipe with your students.

Break matzoh into bite-size pieces. Pour water over matzoh and let soak for two minutes. Gently press excess water from matzoh and transfer to a dry bowl. Add eggs, milk, and salt; then mix. Melt margarine in an electric skillet and add the bowl's contents. Stir occasionally until mixture is set. Serve hot.

AFIKOMAN

At Passover, the leader of the Seder breaks a piece of matzoh in half. The largest piece of broken matzoh is the afikoman and symbolizes the paschal lamb that was a sacrifice to God in thanks for freedom from exile. The afikoman is the last thing eaten at the Seder, and is shared by everyone at the feast. During the Seder, children play a game and search for the afikoman. Re-create this game by wrapping a matzoh in a napkin or towel and hiding it in the classroom. Invite students to search for the matzoh. Invite the student who finds the matzoh to reward the class with treats such as candy or stickers.

FOUR SONS

Explain that the *Haggadah* (the Passover book of prayers and ceremonies) gives examples of four kinds of sons: the wise son, the rebellious son, the simple son, and the son who does not know how to ask. Divide the class into four groups, and assign a kind of son to each group. Name an everyday problem such as *Your parents gave you five dollars to buy lunch for the week. On the way to school you lost the money. What do you do?* Ask groups to brainstorm how each son would handle the problem. Invite groups to share. Next ask groups to brainstorm the consequences each son might face due to his behavior, and have groups share. To close, ask students which son they would most like to be.

SEDER SYMBOLS

1. This is a symbol of the bitterness the Jewish people felt when they were slaves in Egypt.

2. This is a symbol of the mortar the Jewish slaves used to make bricks in Egypt.

3. This is a symbol of God's outstretched arm, helping the Jewish people when they are in trouble.

4. This is a symbol of the cycle of life.

5. This is a symbol of spring and its promise of hope. It also symbolizes Jewish people's faith in the future.

6. This is a symbol of the tears cried by the Israelite slaves.

April © 1997 Creative Teaching Press

SPACE RACE DAY

On April 12, 1961, Cosmonaut Yuri Gagarin helped Russia win the "space race" by becoming the first man in space. He orbited the earth for 108 minutes! But the space race wasn't over. Soon after on July 20, 1969, the United States sent the first man to walk on the moon. Highlight humankind's accomplishments in space by celebrating Space Race Day. It's out of this world!

LITERATURE LINKS

I Want to Be an Astronaut by Byron Barton

Mooncake by Frank Asch

My First Book About Space: A Question and Answer Book by Dinah L. Moche

On the Moon by Jenny Vaughn

Trouble in Space by Rose Greydanus

SPRINGTIME SPACE CREATURE

Explain that the first astronauts had no idea what they might find in space. Ask students to imagine they are the first astronauts and have encountered a "springtime space creature" on a planet called "Aprilite." Invite students to create the creature using art and craft supplies. Display the creatures on a table covered with plastic or paper grass. Title the scene *Springtime in Space.*

MATERIALS

▲ art supplies (construction paper, crayons or markers, paints, paintbrushes, scissors, glue, tape)

▲ craft supplies (plastic or paper flowers, plastic or paper grass, egg cartons, paper sacks, pipe cleaners, springtime stickers)

MATERIALS

▲ *I Want to Be an Astronaut*
   by Byron Barton

▲ Rocket reproducible
   (page 67)

▲ crayons or markers

▲ student photos

▲ scissors

▲ glue

▲ construction paper

▲ page decorators (star
   stickers, rubber
   stamps, glitter, etc.)

▲ bookbinding materials

I'M OUT OF THIS WORLD

Read *I Want to Be an Astronaut* aloud. After story discussion, distribute Rocket reproducibles and crayons or markers. Read the poem on the rocket aloud. Invite students to complete each line. Have students glue their photos in the rocket window and color their rockets. Have students cut out their rockets, glue them to construction paper, and use page decorators to make the rockets look like they are in space. Bind the pages in a class book titled *We're Out of this World.*

MATERIALS

▲ solar system diagram

▲ folder

▲ scissors

▲ colored felt

▲ marker

▲ index cards

▲ flannel board

PLANETS LEARNING CENTER

Using a solar system diagram for a size and color guide, cut a sun and nine planets from felt. Print the name of each planet on its felt shape. Copy each planet's name on a separate word card. Place the solar system diagram in a folder as an answer key. Place the felt planets, word cards, and answer key next to a flannel board as a learning center. Teach students the sentence *My very educated mother just sent us nine pizzas* as a reminder of the planets' order in relation to the sun: Mercury, Venus, Earth, Mars, Jupiter, Saturn, Uranus, Neptune, Pluto. Have student pairs visit the learning center and take turns pulling word cards from a turned-over, mixed-up pile. When a student pulls a card, challenge him or her to place the sun or planet in the correct place on the flannel board. Have students consult the answer key when everything is placed.

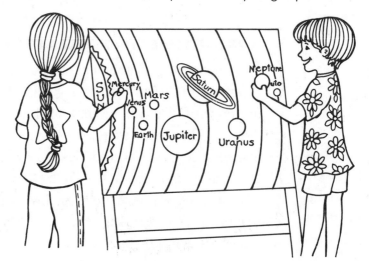

ROCKET

I see _____

I hear _____

I wonder _____

I think _____

I want to _____

I hope _____

I don't _____

I'm out of this world!

DICTIONARY DAY

People became much better spellers on April 14, 1828. This is the date the first edition of Webster's dictionary was released. Celebrate the dictionary and its contents with Dictionary Day. After these fun activities, your students may actually choose to use the dictionary!

LITERATURE LINKS

Agatha's Alphabet, With Her Very Own Dictionary
by Lucy Floyd

The Cat in the Hat Beginner Book Dictionary
by Dr. Seuss

The Magic World of Words
by William D. Halsey

My First Word Book
by Angela Wilkes

Richard Scarry's Biggest Word Book Ever
by Richard Scarry

SPRINGTIME CLASS DICTIONARY

Display a Webster's dictionary and discuss its history and anniversary. Divide the class into groups to create their own dictionaries. Have each group brainstorm a springtime word for each letter of the alphabet. Ask groups to share their words. Distribute a different bulletin-board letter and construction paper to each student. Invite students each to glue the letter to paper and use it as the first letter in a springtime word they write. (Students may use already-shared words or their own.) Have students use crayons or markers and art supplies to decorate around their words. Bind the papers in a class book titled *Springtime Class Dictionary*.

MATERIALS

- ▲ Webster's dictionary
- ▲ writing paper
- ▲ bulletin board letters
- ▲ construction paper
- ▲ glue
- ▲ crayons or markers
- ▲ art supplies (tissue paper, glitter, pipe cleaners, beans, buttons)
- ▲ bookbinding materials

NAME GAME

Look up each student's name in a first-name dictionary or a baby name book. Read the definition of each student's name (or a similar name) aloud. Have each student write his or her name on a slip of paper and place it in a container. If students share a first name, have them write their last initials. Pull out a slip of paper from the container, read the name silently, and then read the definition or origin of that name. Challenge students with that name to stand as quickly as possible. If the student does not recognize the definition of his or her name, or if the wrong student stands, say the first letter of the name. Play the game until all names are drawn.

DICTIONARY HUNT

Divide the class into groups of three and distribute a dictionary, writing paper, and three slips of paper to each. Have groups use the dictionary to think of three questions whose answers can be found in it. For example, a group could ask *What is the meaning of the word* spelunker? or *On what page would you find the word* gnat? Have students write their questions and answers on writing paper and then copy each question on a slip of paper. Place the slips of paper in a container. One at a time, pull out a slip of paper from the container and read the question. Challenge all groups, except the one who wrote the question, to find the answer as quickly as possible. The first group to answer the question correctly receives a point. Continue the game until all questions have been answered. The team with the most points wins.

DA VINCI DAY

April 15

On April 15, 1452, Leonardo da Vinci, the renown artist, inventor, and scientist, was born. To celebrate da Vinci's birthday, invite your students to participate in Leonardo da Vinci Day activities—the day will be a masterpiece!

LITERATURE LINKS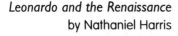

Leonardo and the Renaissance
by Nathaniel Harris

Leonardo da Vinci, the Artist, Inventor, Scientist
by Alice and Martin Provensen

The Painter's Trick
by Piero Ventura

Painting Faces
by Suzanne Haldane

Paints
by Henry Pluckrose

Regina's Big Mistake
by Marissa Moss

MAKE A MASTERPIECE

Explain that Leonardo da Vinci was known for his realistic drawings and paintings. Pass around photographs of da Vinci's work and point out the detailed facial expressions, backgrounds, and bodies. Invite students to imitate da Vinci's style and sketch a replica of a da Vinci painting using pencils or drawing charcoal and construction paper. Have students paint their sketches using oil, acrylic, or tempera paint. Display the paintings in groups next to the "real" paintings they represent.

MATERIALS
▲ photographs of Leonardo da Vinci paintings
▲ pencils or drawing charcoal
▲ construction paper
▲ oil, acrylic, or tempera paints/paintbrushes

BACKWARD STORY

MATERIALS

▲ picture book with sequential events
▲ construction paper
▲ crayons or markers
▲ bookbinding materials

Explain that to hide his ideas from spies, Leonardo da Vinci wrote his notes backward. Tell students they will soon practice "thinking backward," and should listen carefully as you read a story aloud. Read the picture book aloud. Divide students into groups and give each group enough construction paper to represent each main event in the story. Invite groups to use crayons and markers to illustrate each main event. Ask groups to sequence the finished drawings backward. Flip through the books from back to front so groups can check the sequencing. Invite groups to rearrange the papers if necessary and bind them into group books entitled *Storytelling Backward to Forward*.

DESIGN A FORTRESS

MATERIALS

▲ drawing paper
▲ tissue boxes
▲ art supplies (glue, tape, construction paper, scissors, crayons or markers, plastic or paper objects)

Explain that Leonardo da Vinci not only painted, he was a scientist, inventor, and architect. Explain that da Vinci thought of and made detailed sketches of modern-day helicopters, parachutes, machine guns, and fortresses. Ask students to be like da Vinci and invent a fortress. Tell students they can add anything they wish to their fortresses to keep out enemies. Have students sketch and label their ideas on drawing paper. Once sketches are drawn, invite students to create three-dimensional models of their fortresses using art supplies. Display the fortresses and invite other classes to tour the room.

SILENT DAY

April 16

Charlie Chaplin, the silent film star, was born on April 16, 1889. To have a little fun and perhaps actually hear those April showers tapping on your classroom window pane, have a day full of silent activities. The following will get you started!

LITERATURE LINKS

The Cat Who Lost His Purr
by Michele Coxon

Charlie Chaplin
by Gloria Karnen

Just Listen
by Winifred Morris

My Sister's Silent World
by Catherine Arthur

Soft and Noisy
by Judy HIndley

SILENT FILM

Discuss Charlie Chaplin and silent films. Show a short silent film to the class and point out how dialogue and narration were shown in words that viewers had to read. Invite students to create a silent film about one of their favorite stories. Have the class vote to choose a story, and assign parts. Invite the class to make or choose props. Practice miming the story. Have a "word team" create posters with dialogue and narration to show between scenes. Have students perform and record the silent film on videocassette. Make popcorn and invite another class and parents to watch the film. Send the film home each night with a different student so family members can watch it.

MATERIALS

▲ silent-film videocassette
▲ VCR
▲ props (hats, costumes, everyday objects)
▲ poster board
▲ markers
▲ video camera
▲ blank videocassette
▲ popcorn

SILENT PUZZLES

MATERIALS

▲ age-appropriate puzzles

Discuss ways to communicate other than talking and writing, such as through eye contact or hand and body gestures. Divide the class into groups of three. Challenge each group to complete a puzzle without speaking. Invite groups to use hand and body gestures to communicate. After puzzles are complete, ask questions such as *Was it difficult to put the puzzle together? Why? What did your group do to communicate? What other senses did you have to use to understand your group? How do you think people who cannot hear or talk communicate?*

CHARLIE CHAPLIN TIME

MATERIALS

▲ scissors
▲ Charlie Chaplin Button reproducible (page 74)
▲ safety pins

Photocopy and cut out several Charlie Chaplin buttons. On Silent Day, explain that whenever you say *Charlie Chaplin*, the class should become instantly quiet and "freeze" in position. Explain that you will give a button to students who can remain quiet and "frozen" for at least 20 seconds. Say the "magic words" two or three times in the morning and distribute buttons. Invite students to attach safety pins to the buttons and wear them. Change the game after two or three practices; give buttons as rewards for students who remain quiet during quiet work time.

CHARLIE CHAPLIN BUTTONS

EARTH DAY

Earth Day brings awareness of environmental concerns and the need for conservation. Help your students gain a greater appreciation and sense of responsibility for the earth by having them complete the following Earth Day activities—they're educational and fun!

LITERATURE LINKS

Acorn Alone
by Michael McClure

The Clean Brook
by Margaret F. Bartlett

The Earth and I
by Frank Asch

Mother Earth
by Nancy Luenn

Oil Spill
by Melvin Berger

Recycle!
by Gail Gibbons

Where Does the Garbage Go?
by Paul Showers

The Wump World
by Bill Peet

EARTH DAY QUILT BULLETIN BOARD

Read *Mother Earth* aloud. After discussing the need to preserve our natural resources, have students brainstorm things they can do to help the earth. Have each student turn a white paper square so a corner is at the top, making a diamond shape. Invite each student to illustrate his or her idea on the diamond with crayons or markers. Have students glue their illustrations to colored construction-paper squares. Have each student write a sentence describing the picture in the construction-paper border surrounding the illustration. Staple the illustrations in a quilt design on a bulletin board, using construction-paper squares as "filler" between illustrations. Title the bulletin board *An Earth Day Quilt*.

MATERIALS

▲ *Mother Earth* by Nancy Luenn
▲ 6" (15.5 cm) white paper squares
▲ crayons or markers
▲ glue
▲ 9" (23 cm) colored construction-paper squares
▲ 9" (23 cm) black construction-paper squares
▲ stapler

TRASH-EATING MONSTERS

Discuss the harmful effects of litter and ways to minimize it. Distribute a lunch sack to each student. Invite students to use art supplies and decorate their sacks to look like trash-eating monsters. Divide the class into teams. Challenge team members to pick up trash around the school and feed their monsters until the sacks are as full as possible. Assemble the teams and invite students to estimate how many large, plastic trash bags of trash were collected. Have each student dump the trash into the large bags. Compare the estimation with the actual number.

EARTH DAY PICNIC

In advance, write a note on April border pages asking parents to pack an Earth Day lunch for their child. Explain that Earth Day lunches are special and should be made creatively, and with the environment in mind. For example, students can carry lunches in biodegradable wrappings (rather than plastic) or use reusable containers (such as thermoses rather than juice boxes). Challenge parents to send natural foods that are free from preservatives. On Earth Day, take students outside. Invite students to discuss their foods and the creative ways they are packaged. Have students throw away their trash in the same trash can. Discuss how little trash is in the container in comparison to everyday lunch trash.

THE EARTH UP CLOSE

Take students to a nearby wooded area, meadow, or field. Have each student choose a favorite spot and lay a yarn strand in a circle on the ground. Ask students to use magnifying glasses to observe the earth inside the circles for 5 to 10 minutes. Invite students to move things they observe to examine what is under them. Discuss student observations. Ask questions such as *What living things were inside your circle? What did you notice after several minutes of looking that you didn't notice at first? What looked more interesting under a magnifying glass? Which animals and insects depend on things growing in your circle? Why is it important to take care of the earth?*

REUSE IT!

Read *Recycle!* aloud. Discuss recycling and the variety of ways it can be done. Discuss how people can reuse everyday items in new ways before throwing them away or recycling them. Display a pile of not-so-messy everyday trash. Invite each student to select an item from the pile, tell what it is made of, and explain one way it can be reused before being recycled.

DO WE NEED IT?

Display a wrapped package of mini-boxed raisins and a large box of raisins. Have students discuss why they might choose one kind over the other. Ask, *Which package probably holds more raisins? Why?* Pour the contents of all the mini-boxes into one bowl and the large box into another. Discuss the amount of trash created by each packaging style. Place each bowl on one end of a balance scale and compare the weights. Ask, *Which bowl is heavier? Why?* Divide the class into two teams. Ask each team to count the number of raisins in a bowl. Have teams report numbers. Ask, *Which bowl had more raisins? Based on this information, which packaging creates the most waste? If you were shopping for raisins, which packaging would you choose? Why? How can you help the earth and still carry a small amount of raisins in your lunch?*

EARTH DAY GLOBES

Display a globe and point out the seven continents. To make personal Earth Day globes, invite each student to stuff crushed newspaper into a paper grocery sack. Ask students to mold the sacks into round shapes and tie the tops with twist ties or bread tabs. Have students paint the bags blue. When dry, have students color the Continents reproducible, cut out the continents, and glue them to the sacks in the correct positions. Invite each student to write *It's Our World. Let's Take Care of It.* on one index card and *Earth Day* (and the year) on the other. Have each student glue the cards back-to-back to cover the bag's "stem." Hang the globes from the classroom ceiling or in the auditorium as an Earth Day decoration.

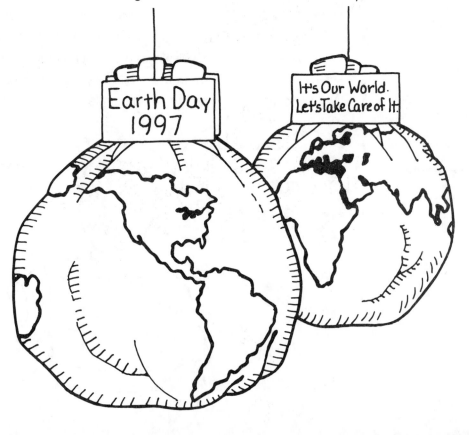

CONTINENTS

ARBOR DAY

April 22

Arbor Day began in 1872 when news editor Julius Sterling Morton, who realized that trees enrich the soil and conserve moisture, began to plant trees.

Celebrate Arbor Day by planting a tree and completing the following Arbor Day activities—your students' appreciation for nature, like the planted tree, will grow and grow!

LITERATURE LINKS

Cherry Tree
by Ruskin Bond

The Giving Tree
by Shel Silverstein

In My Treehouse
by Alice Schertle

The Lorax
by Dr. Seuss

Redwoods Are the Tallest Trees in the World
by David A. Adler

Sing a Song of Popcorn selected by Beatrice Schenk de Regniers

I-LOVE-APRIL TREE

Obtain a potted tree from a garden center for a class tree. The week before Arbor Day, discuss the month of April and things that symbolize it, such as rain, flowers, rabbits, chicks, and wind. Invite students to create "April ornaments" for your class tree using art and craft supplies. Place the ornaments on the tree. Leave the ornaments on the tree until Arbor Day. On Arbor Day, take the tree outside and have the class plant it. Invite a student to read the poem "Our Tree" as a dedication to the tree.

MATERIALS

- ▲ potted tree
- ▲ art supplies (construction paper, crayons or markers, scissors, glue)
- ▲ craft supplies (plastic or paper flowers, aluminum foil, string, pipe cleaners, cupcake liners, cotton balls)
- ▲ gardening tools (shovel, trowels, gloves)
- ▲ soil
- ▲ "Our Tree" by Marchette Chute (from *Sing a Song of Popcorn*)

HUG A TREE

MATERIALS

▲ school-yard or neighborhood tree

▲ fertilizer

▲ mulch or peat moss

▲ flowers

▲ water

▲ gardening tools (shovel, trowels, gloves)

Discuss the need to take care of trees because of the oxygen, soil protection, and beauty they give. As a class, adopt a tree to take care of and "hug" for the rest of the school year. First, have students "hug" the tree with fertilizer. Next, have them "hug" the tree with mulch or peat moss. Finally, have students "hug" the tree with a ring of flowers. Each week, invite students to water and fertilize the tree and pull weeds and rake leaves near it. At the end of the year, take the class outside and read a favorite picture book under the tree.

"LEAF" IT TO ME

MATERIALS

▲ brown butcher paper

▲ stapler

▲ scissors

▲ crayons or markers

▲ construction paper

▲ tape

Create a floor-to-ceiling paper tree trunk and branches by twisting brown butcher paper into wrinkled cylinders. Staple the tree trunk and branches to a corner wall. Invite students each to think of one thing they can do to take care of the trees in their yards or neighborhoods, such as water them, rake leaves, or avoid nailing or tying things to them. Invite each student to design, decorate near them, and cut out a large construction-paper leaf. Ask each student to write a caretaking suggestion on one side of the leaf and **Leaf It to Me** on the other. Invite students to tape their leaves to the paper tree branches. Near the tree, display the title **Leaf It to Me to Take Care of a Tree!**

NEWSPAPER DAY

April 24

April 24 marks the day the United States' first newspaper was published. *The Boston News Letter* sold its first issue on that date in 1704. Celebrate the birth of our news by participating in Newspaper Day activities—they're hot off the presses and ready to go!

LITERATURE LINKS

Deadline! From News to Newspaper
by Gail Gibbons

The Furry News: How to Make a Newspaper
by Loreen Leedy

Hot Off the Press! A Day at the Daily News
by Margaret Miller

How to Read a Newspaper
by Helen Carey and Judith Greenberg

Running a School Newspaper
by Vivian Dubrovin

HAVING FUN WITH HEADLINES

Cut out an interesting newspaper headline for each student. Place headlines in a container and invite each student to take one. Ask each student to glue his or her headline to a piece of construction paper. Invite each student to invent a newspaper story to go with the headline and illustrate it on the paper. Have each student write (or dictate as you write) the story on writing paper and attach the paper below the illustration. Invite students to read and share their stories and illustrations. Display the news stories under the title *Extra! Extra! Read All About It!*

MATERIALS

▲ scissors
▲ interesting newspaper headlines
▲ container
▲ glue
▲ construction paper
▲ crayons or markers
▲ writing paper

SCAVENGER HUNT

Divide the class into teams of four. Distribute a newspaper, Scavenger Hunt reproducible, piece of construction paper, and glue to each team. Provide each team member with scissors. Explain the reproducible directions and the items on the scavenger hunt list. Give teams 30 minutes to find newspaper items, cut them out, glue them to the construction paper, and complete the reproducible. Explain that the goal is not to be the first team finished, but to complete the reproducible within 30 minutes. Discuss team results and what students learned about the newspaper and working with a group.

HOMEMADE PRINTING PRESS

In advance, mix unflavored gelatin with half the recommended amount of water in a cake pan. Refrigerate for the recommended length of time and set aside. Have the class brainstorm newsworthy classroom events, such as field trips or class projects. Divide the class into groups of three. Have each group write or dictate a classroom-event article. Edit articles and have groups copy them on "ditto masters." Have groups peel away the part of the "ditto master" with ink. Bring out the cake pan and dampen the gelatin. Have one group lay the inked paper on the gelatin, gently press, and peel away, leaving ink behind. (The words should be backward.) Have the group lay a blank piece of drawing paper on the ink, gently press, and peel to reveal a "photocopy" of the article. Have the group repeat the process until an article is made for each group. (Students may have to wipe the ink away when it dries out and wet the surface again from time to time.) Invite each group to make copies of its article using the gelatin. Staple the articles to create booklets and provide one newspaper for each group.

MATERIALS

▲ newspapers
▲ scissors
▲ glue
▲ Help Wanted
  reproducible (page 86)

HELP WANTED

Invite each student to complete a Help Wanted reproducible by reviewing a help-wanted newspaper section, cutting out advertisements, and gluing the advertisements to the reproducible. After completion, divide the class into groups to discuss their answers.

MATERIALS

▲ newspapers
▲ scissors
▲ glue
▲ construction paper
▲ calculators

ON SALE

Invite each student to look through newspaper advertisements and make a "wish list" of items he or she would like to purchase. Explain that the goal is to "spend" as close to $1,000.00 as possible. Have students cut out items and their listed cost and glue them on construction paper. Have each student add his or her total with a calculator and record next to the items the sum and the difference between the sum and $1,000.00. Invite students to share their wish lists and totals. As a variation for younger students, have them find items that add to $50.00 or $100.00.

NEWSPAPER SCAVENGER HUNT

Team Members:

_____

Your goals are

- to cooperate and participate.
- to be organized, finding the most items in the least amount of time.
- to find, cut out, glue to paper, and check off as many items as possible in 30 minutes.

You are hunting for

- ❏ the title of the newspaper.
- ❏ the largest headline on the first page of the sports section.
- ❏ a comic strip.
- ❏ the television schedule.
- ❏ the date.
- ❏ the weather map.
- ❏ the crossword puzzle.
- ❏ a help-wanted advertisement.
- ❏ the index.
- ❏ a movie advertisement.
- ❏ an article about another country.

TEAM SELF-EVALUATION	Almost Always	Sometimes	Never
Did everyone help?			
Were we organized?			
Did we follow directions?			
Did everyone try his or her best?			

HELP WANTED

Name _____

Cut out a help-wanted advertisement for each category and glue one advertisement in each box.

This is a job I would *love* to have.	This is a job I would *not* like.	This is a job that probably pays *a lot* of money.
This is a job that probably pays a *little* money.	This is a job that seems "too good to be true."	This is a job that seems like hard work.

FROG DAY

In April, the weather warms and hibernating animals rise from their slumber. Waking up with the other animals is a "springy" symbol of spring—the frog! Hold a Frog Day in your classroom to create a perfect blend of science and season. The following activities will get you started.

LITERATURE LINKS

The Caterpillar and the Polliwog
by Jack Kent

The Frog
by Paula Hogan

"Frog and Toad" series
by Arnold Lobel

Froggy Gets Dressed
by Jonathan London

Let's Go, Froggy
by Jonathan London

Little Frog's Song
by Alice Schertle

Rra-ah
by Eros Keith

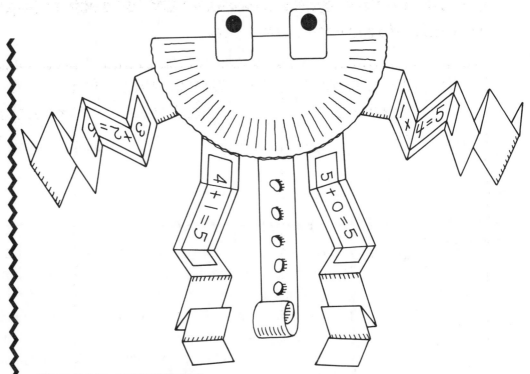

FROGGY ADDITION

Have each student paint the back of a paper plate green. Have each student fold the plate in half so a green half-circle "frog body" shows. Ask each student to fold two file-folder labels over the plate's crease so approximately 1/2" (1.5 cm) of each label is above the paper plate. Ask students to draw eyes in the labels. Have students accordion-fold four green construction-paper strips. Have students glue the strips between the circle halves, hanging down from the sides, to represent frog legs. Have each student glue a red construction-paper "tongue" between the halves, down the center of the frog, and then glue the plates closed. Invite each student to glue several black-bean "flies" on the frog's tongue. Distribute four file-folder labels to each student. Ask each student to write an addition problem on each label that adds to the number of flies on the tongue. Have students attach the labels to the frog legs.

MATERIALS
- ▲ paper plates
- ▲ green tempera paint/paintbrushes
- ▲ adhesive file-folder labels
- ▲ markers
- ▲ glue
- ▲ 1"x 12" (2.5 cm x 31 cm) green and red construction-paper strips
- ▲ black beans
- ▲ scissors
- ▲ fishing line

LIFE CYCLE SONG

Read *The Caterpillar and the Polliwog* aloud and discuss the life cycle of a frog. To reinforce learning, teach students the following song and motions. Practice the song and perform it for parents or other classes.

Polliwog	Motions
(to the tune of "Are You Sleeping?")	
Pol-li-wog (clap), pol-li-wog (clap).	*Students move hands in swimming motion and clap twice.*
Lost your tail, lost your tail.	*Students pull imaginary tail off twice.*
Look, you've got two feet.	*Students hold up two fingers and point to toes.*
Look, you've got four feet.	*Students hold up four fingers and point to toes.*
Now you're a frog.	*Students hop like frogs.*
Now you're a frog.	*Students hop like frogs.*

LEAPING LILY PADS

MATERIALS

▲ nonfiction book about frogs
▲ green construction paper
▲ marker
▲ scissors
▲ tape
▲ die

Use several facts from a "frog book" to create 20 questions. Write each question on a separate piece of green construction paper. Cut out large lily-pad shapes around the questions. Tape each lily pad to the floor in a line. Read the frog book aloud. Divide the class into two teams. Choose a student from each team to be a "leapfrog" for the first round. Have another student from each team roll the die. Ask the leapfrogs to hop from pad to pad until they hop to the number rolled. Ask the question on that lily pad. Invite team members to conference and give an answer to the question. If their answer is correct, the leapfrog's team stays on that lily pad. If the answer is incorrect or unknown, the leapfrog goes back one space. Replace leapfrogs after each question is asked so every student has a chance to hop. Ask questions until one team leaps off the pads.

APRIL

SUNDAY	MONDAY	TUESDAY	WEDNESDAY	THURSDAY	FRIDAY	SATURDAY

Raindrops and Umbrellas Border

Bunnies and Chicks Border

April News